About the Title of this Book

Most translations of the Great Commission (Matthew 28:18-20) render it as if we are commanded to go. In the original Greek, the imperative is to *make disciples*. The word *go* could be translated, *"as you are going."* While God may send you to a particular place to fulfill a particular ministry, as a Christian, you have been called to witness for Jesus Christ wherever you are right now, and for the rest of your life. So, wherever you are going, whenever you are going, and for whatever reason you are going, the assignment Jesus gave you is always the same:

As you are going ... Make Disciples

Bob Prall

As You are Going ... Make Disciples

Robert L. Prall, M.Div

Emmaus Books Trust
Houston, Texas

ISBN 0-9657835-4-5

Quantity prices are available
upon request by sending an e-mail to
books@hisbride.org

Emmaus Books Trust web page
www.HisBride.org

Cover design by Randy Thompson
Artec, Houston, Texas

Table of Contents

Forward

I met Bob Prall during my freshman year at Duke University. He was the director of Campus Crusade for Christ in North Carolina, and I came to know Christ as my Savior through my involvement with the Campus Crusade students and staff on the Duke campus. The following is from an article I wrote for Moody Magazine that tells the rest of the story:

Churches that Equip
by Rusty Wright

I still remember the sinking feeling in the pit of my stomach. I was a university student, a young believer, and my faith in Christ seemed like a house of cards that had just crumbled. For awhile, the Christian life that had been so exciting and joyful became a myth. I felt rootless, adrift, and confused.

One of my fraternity brothers had just asked me some questions about Christianity that I couldn't answer. This bothered me deeply until Bob Prall, a pastor and campus Christian worker, answered them for me. "Always remember," he advised as he finished, "just because you don't know the answer, doesn't mean there is no answer."

For the next two years I followed him around, watching as he shared Christ with skeptics, listening to his speeches, and observing how he dealt with non-Christians. Bob's loving, learned example and teaching helped me sink my spiritual roots deeply into God's truth and provided a foundation for three decades of interaction with unbelievers. I shall always be grateful to him for equipping me in this way.

Moody Magazine, April/May 1999 Issue

Let me commend to you Bob's book *As You are going ... Make Disciples*. I trust that there will be some who read this book who will profit from it, just as I did when I was Bob's "Timothy" many years ago.

Rusty Wright, Traveling Lecturer
International School of Theology
Mount Hermon, California

Introduction

In the fall of 1958, as a Second Lieutenant in the Army, I attended the Infantry School at Fort Benning, Georgia. After so many years, I do not recall a lot of what they taught us, but I do recall them telling us about a study the Army did on our combat troops in Korea.

In this study, the Army found that, in the heat of battle, only ten to twenty percent of the riflemen would pull the trigger. To the Army's dismay, their study found that it was not unusual for one man to provide the entire firepower from an eleven-man rifle squad.

These findings mystified the Army brass, and they conducted numerous surveys to endeavor to find the reasons why. While many men were not willing to admit their reasons for holding their fire, the study came up with a variety of explanations.

Some men said they could never spot a good target. Some felt that they were not very good marksmen, so why bother. Others were afraid they might kill someone, and the thought was terrifying. Others were afraid that the enemy might spot where the gunfire was coming from and shoot back. Many were just plain scared.

I recently shared this with a pastor and commented that the Army's experience in Korea is a picture of today's Church. He quickly responded, "If we had ten to twenty percent of our people witnessing, we would have a great revival." Sadly, his observation is probably correct. It is likely that the U.S. Army in Korea had a higher percentage of its soldiers pulling the trigger than the typical church has members who tell other people the good news about Jesus. We need to ask why.

My guess is that some believers, who want to witness, rarely recognize it when they have a golden opportunity. Others feel that they don't have enough knowledge to be effective in presenting the Gospel. Others are afraid that they will be asked tough questions that they cannot answer, and others are just plain scared of witnessing. The saddest part of this is that many Christians are missing out on one of the greatest blessing in their lives -- seeing God use them as an instrument to help others come to know their Savior.

The goal of this book is to help believers overcome impediments to sharing their faith. Just as a soldier needs to be trained to be effective in battle, so also Christians need training to be effective witnesses for Jesus Christ. This book is a compilation of things I have learned, and have found effective, in some thirty-eight years of personal witnessing. You might call reading and digesting this book, "A Boot Camp for a Christian Witness." But, just as the training of a soldier continues on after boot camp, so also, as Christian witnesses we need refreshers to keep us effective and motivated. I trust that this book will serve that purpose for those who already effective witnesses and are *making disciples... as they are going.*

While some Christian evidences are presented in this book, the information provided is not exhaustive. Consequently, some scholars may read this book and conclude that it is incomplete, as it does not attempt to answer every question and objection one might face when witnessing. Please understand, this books is purposefully limited in its scope. It is what I call pragmatic, practical, strategic evangelism and apologetics (defense of the faith and Christian evidences). Pragmatic, because I don't think we should waste our time dealing with issues that either don't matter, or will merely distract us from having an effective witness for Jesus. Practical, because it will show how to give clear and concise explanations of Christian evidences without going into great detail. Strategic, as if focuses on having a planned strategy as we endeavor to tell people the Good News about Jesus.

We are in a battle for the minds of men and women. My prayer is that this book will help equip and motivate its readers to be more effective as soldiers for Jesus Christ, and that many men and women will come to know Jesus Christ as their Savior as a result of their witnesses for Him. What a time it will be in glory when we all rejoice in the presence of Jesus.

Some words of encouragement from the Scriptures -- as you begin reading this book

For no man can lay a foundation other than the one which is laid, which is Jesus Christ. Now if any man builds upon the foundation with gold, silver, precious stones, wood, hay, straw, each man's work will become evident; for the day will show it, because it is to be revealed with fire; and the fire will test the quality of each man's work. If any man's work which he has built upon it remains, he shall receive a reward.

I Corinthians 3:11-14

And many of those who sleep in the dust of the ground will awake, these to everlasting life, but the others to disgrace and everlasting contempt. And those who have insight will shine brightly like the expanse of heaven, and those who lead many to righteousness, like the stars forever and ever.

Daniel 12:2-3

Chapter One

Lessons from the Sixties

Behold, I say to you, lift up your eyes, and look on the fields, that they are white for harvest.

Jesus, John 4:35

In the spring of 1961, a few years after graduating from the University of Oregon, I accepted Jesus Christ as my Savior. About six months later, I enrolled at Western Baptist Seminary in Portland, Oregon. November 22, 1963, during my last year in seminary, our chapel service was interrupted with the news that President John F. Kennedy had been shot in Dallas.

It was almost like that tragic event was the kick-off for a decade of turmoil in America. The war in Vietnam heated up, and during the following years, our country had three more assassinations of well known political figures, as Malcolm X, Martin Luther King, Jr., and Bobby Kennedy were also gunned down.

The anti-war demonstrations on our college campuses became so confrontational between students and the police that students referred to the police as "pigs" because of the snouts on the gas masks they wore when they used tear gas to disburse rowdy crowds. During an anti-war protest demonstration at Kent State University, police gunfire tragically killed four students.

As a result of these and other factors, a large youth subculture developed in America. Dr. Timothy Leary, a psychology professor at Harvard University, promoted LSD and urged the youth of America to "tune in, turn on, and drop out." And drop out they did. Many became longhaired hippies who lived together in drug-infested communes and advocated a promiscuous sexual revolution.

The depiction of the generation gap between Archie Bunker and Mike Stivic (whom Archie always called Meathead) in the popular TV sitcom "All in the Family," was funny because it was a caricature of what was happening in living rooms across the land. The older generations assumed that many of the younger generation had become communist kooks, and a common saying among the disgruntled youth was "Don't trust anyone over thirty."

Religion in America was also in turmoil. The Beatles claimed that they were more popular than Jesus Christ, and many people believed them. In 1963, a best selling book titled *Honest to God*, by Bishop John A.T. Robonson, announced that the Church in America had become irrelevant, and a few years later the best seller was a book by Thomas Altizer and William Hamilton, who wrote an obituary for God. Time Magazine jumped on their theological bandwagon and published an issue with a front cover that proclaimed, "God is Dead."

A Time Magazine cover in the Sixties parroted a proclamation that God is Dead.

Upon graduation from seminary in 1964, I wanted to go where the action was, so I joined the staff of Campus Crusade for Christ. At that time, Campus Crusade was still a small organization with a total worldwide staff of just under 300.

That year, Campus Crusade purchased an old resort hotel in San Bernardino, California called Arrowhead Springs. It was a great facility, and an outstanding place to train college students in evangelism. Our motto was "Win the campus today, and win the world tomorrow." To accomplish that objective, we invited Christian college students to come to Arrowhead Springs for Leadership Training Institutes (called LTI's for short).

At these institutes, Dr. Bill Bright delivered a five-message series, and we had rotating small group seminars where we taught the students how to share their faith. The Four Spiritual Laws were not yet in booklet form, and we had the students memorize them, the supporting scripture verses, and the diagrams. We witnessed by writing the Four Spiritual Laws, including the verse references and the diagrams, on a sheet of paper, or on the back of an evangelistic letter by Dr. Bright, called the Van Dusen Letter. But, they frequently ended up on the back of a coffee shop napkin.

Knowing that these students needed to build up their confidence before they returned to their campuses, we wanted to give them some positive witnessing experiences. Most of these LTI's had at least 500 students, and, as facilities were added at Arrowhead Springs, the numbers grew to where some included about 1,500 students. Consequently, we needed to find a lot of people who were receptive to having a conversation with a stranger. The beaches of Orange County, about an hour away, were obvious locations where people were relaxing and would be happy to talk to a stranger if approached tastefully.

All summer long, one or two days every week, we would give the students sack lunches, equip them with clipboards, religious surveys, and copies of the Van Dusen Letter, load them in cars, and head for the beaches. Sometimes we joked about singing, "Onward clipboard soldiers, marching to the beach, where are all those atheists, we are out to reach."

Frankly, I did not like going to the beach, and I am sure that some other staff members felt the same way. As a young man, I had enough problems with my eyes without going to bikini beach. Furthermore, I did not have a suntan, and either I was going to be one of the few pure white bodies on the beach and get burned to a crisp, or I would be one of the few people on the beach wearing a sweatshirt.

Week after week, all summer long, we evangelized those beaches with from 500 to 1,500 Christian college students. After many "invasions" of those beaches it was hard to find someone to whom we had not witnessed several times. During those summers, there was probably more person to person witnessing per square foot of sand on the Orange County beaches than on any other parcel of real estate in the history of the world, including Jerusalem in the first century.

While I knew that there were going to be individuals who came to know Christ as a result of this witnessing, I did not think that we would greatly impact their communities as there was no effective way to follow up those who prayed to accept Christ. On the other hand, I knew that we needed to give our students some practical experience before they returned to the skeptical wolves on their campuses.

It was always exciting to return to Arrowhead Springs at the end of a day at the beaches. After dinner we had a sharing time, and student after student would excitedly tell of their witnessing experiences. Many would relate that it was the first time they ever had someone pray with them to receive the Lord.

I must admit that at times I was a bit skeptical. During the sharing times, some students would tell how they had lead two or three people to Christ, and I would say to myself, "Sure, they went down there and they were so scared their knees didn't knock, they missed. They found some junior high kids to witness to, and anyone can pressure a junior high kid to pray. But little will come from this because there is no effective follow up." But, our goal was to build up their confidence, and I prayed that good things would happen back on the campuses as a result of their beach experiences.

During the summer of 1966, many of us on the Campus Crusade staff read a book titled, *The Principles of War*. This book talked about applying military tactics to evangelism. One of the tactics the author espoused was that Christians should follow the example of generals who often concentrate their troops at one point on a battlefield so they can have a breakthrough that will have a psychological impact on the whole war.

After reading *The Principles of War*, someone came up with a brainstorm and presented it at a campus directors meeting: "Why not take our entire staff for a week at the University of California at Berkeley, witness to every student on campus, and see if we can have a big spiritual breakthrough that will resonate on campuses all over the country, and ultimately all over the world?" The idea was so exciting that we almost jumped up and down like a bunch of football players ready to play in the Super Bowl. With great enthusiasm, we decided to have our whole staff travel to Berkeley for a week of witnessing, and the following week to go on to Los Angeles and repeat it at UCLA.

The University of California at Berkeley had been repeatedly in the national news because of a near riot when the university administration tried to shut down the student's free speech platform on the steps of the administration building, Sproul Hall. During a massive anti-administration demonstration, Mario Savio, a University of California student, jumped on the top of a police car, and rallied the students to stand up against the administration. That night, Mario made the six-o'clock news on TV, and he became an instant star in the student world across America.

That occurrence gave birth to a student uprising called "The Free Speech Movement." By the time we invaded Berkeley, The Free Speech Movement had degenerated into "The Filthy Speech Movement," and Berkeley had become notorious as a haven for left wing radicals within the student body, and for non-student activists and hippies from the subculture.

In some ways, the campus and surroundings at Berkeley had become a zoo. On the big plaza next to Sproul Hall, there were tables set up to sell buttons with gross sayings such as "Let's lock loins" and "If it feels good, let's do it." There was also a table, with young women sitting behind it, where you could sign up to join the "Sexual Freedom League" and check off appropriate boxes on the application if you were interested in nude parties, mate swapping, and seduction classes. Telegraph Avenue, a street leading to the campus, was second only to the Haight-Ashbury section of nearby San Francisco as a gathering place for the hippies who had dropped out of society.

To accomplish our mission, a team of 70 staff members was assigned to Berkeley for the whole school year. Their assignment for fall semester was to do organizational work and to prepare the way for the whole staff's arrival by lining up speaking engagements for us all over the campus. Our invasion of the campus was scheduled for January, and the 70-man team was to stay for the rest of the year to do follow up. This was a considerable commitment of manpower, as that year the total Campus Crusade for Christ staff, including headquarters staff, numbered only about six hundred. But, we felt that this strategy was justified in light of the potential widespread impact.

As we made our plans, we knew that we would get negative editorials in the student newspapers, and expected "The Berkeley Barb," a radical newspaper that was distributed on Telegraph Avenue, to ridicule us. But that did not deter us, as we assumed that persecution went with the territory. We were not surprised when they quickly labeled us "The God Squad."

***The Berkeley Barb* sarcastically labeled us "The God Squad."**

In God's providence, the Saturday night before the big week, Ronald Reagan, as Governor of California, fired Clark Kerr, the University of California chancellor. Needless to say, that guaranteed a big crowd at the free speech platform on the Sproul Hall steps the following Monday, noon, as the radicals considered Reagan an establishment enemy. But, guess who had the free speech platform reserved. You better believe it, and we were not about to give it up.

In January of 1967, we arrived 602 strong to present the Gospel to the Cal students. We had 600 of our staff and 2 other evangelists to help us saturate the campus with the Gospel. One was Billy Graham, and the other was Hubert Lindsey.

You have undoubtedly heard of Billy Graham, but you may not have heard of Hubert Lindsey. I will never forget when I first spotted him. We had a planning session in the Student Union across from Sproul Plaza on Monday morning. At noon, as I left the building to go to our kick-off at the free speech platform, there, on the sidewalk between Telegraph Avenue and the Sproul Hall Plaza, was Hubert Lindsey.

He was missing several front teeth, had sandy red hair, freckles on top of freckles, and had a battery pack on his back for a portable loud speaker that he was using to preach on the Song of Solomon. His English was not the best, and his questionable grammar was magnified by his country accent. My first response was "Oh no! God, how could you let this happen? What is this hick doing here, this week, at Berkeley?"

What I did not realize was that Hubert Lindsey, affectionately known as Holy Hubert by the Cal students, was there every day. You could say he was just part of the Berkeley landscape.

Hubert did not have an impressive graduate degree, but he did have the entire New Testament memorized and about one third of the Old Testament. And, he really knew his apologetics. Large groups of students would often gather around him to see if they could trap him. Someone would say, "Hubert, doesn't the Bible say so and so?" Hubert would answer, "That's not exactly what it says," and he would quote it correctly off the top of his head.

I became fascinated with Holy Hubert. One afternoon, I watched Him as a group of about 50 students gathered around him to ask him questions. One student said, "Hubert, the Bible says to love your enemy. What if someone took a shot at you?" Hubert replied, "That happened once." The student asked, "Well, what happened?" Hubert responded, "I prayed for the guy, and he became a Christian."

The student then pulled out a jack knife, put it right under Hubert's chin and asked, "What if someone came at you with a knife and said he was going to cut your throat?" Hubert again replied, "That has happened to me too." The student again asked, "Well, what happened?" To that Hubert responded, "I prayed for him, and he became a Christian." Hubert then extended his left arm and asked, "Here, would you like to try cutting off my arm?" The crowd roared with laughter, Holy Hubert had prevailed in another skirmish, and I concluded that God had sent "a Jeremiah" to the Berkeley campus.

I spent some time with Hubert, and he told me that he did not see much fruit in his ministry, that not many people accepted Christ with him. But, Hubert understood his role. He described himself as a rock crusher who crushed the rocks so that others could come along and pick up the gems. As the Apostle Paul explained, **"Some plant, some water, but God gives the increase"** (I Corinthians 3:6-8 paraphrase). I will never forget Hubert, and I am confident that he will shine like a star in Glory. (Daniel 12:2-3.)

At the beginning of our week, every place you went on campus, you could hear people talking about the firing of Dr. Clark Kerr. I don't know that we talked to every student at Berkeley, but we tried our best to do so, and by the end of the week, the buzz on campus was no longer about Clark Kerr. Everyplace you went, you would hear people talking about Jesus Christ.

I remember spending three or four hours, over two days, with a graduate student who had his undergraduate degree from the University of Idaho. After sharing the Gospel with him, answering questions, and presenting Christian evidences, I finally asked him, "What more can I share with you?" He responded, "You have given me more information than I need. I guess from here on out, it is up to me."

He did not accept Christ with me that week, but I knew that he understood the Gospel when we parted. I have lost track of him, and I don't know if he ever trusted in Jesus. He is high on my list of people to check on when I get to heaven.

The climax of the week was Friday at noon when Billy Graham spoke in a large outdoor amphitheater called The Greek Theater. As the students were leaving class, Holy Hubert, with his portable loud speaker, was faithfully encouraging everyone to go up to The Greek Theater to hear Billy Graham.

Our goal was for a spiritual breakthrough at Berkeley like that envisioned in *The Principles of War*.

We prayed that God would give us a big breakthrough at Berkeley like that envisioned in *The Principles of War*. In retrospect, I guess we were not very good military tacticians. If a general wants to have a breakthrough, he does not concentrate his troops at the enemy's strongest point, and there is no doubt that in those days, Berkeley was one of Satan's strongest bastions. There were many who did come to know Jesus as their Savior as a result of that exciting week, and there is no doubt that the Berkeley campus was saturated with the Gospel. But, we did not have a breakthrough that greatly impacted other campuses, our nation, and the whole world.

A few months later there was a big spiritual breakthrough that originated in California and impacted the nation. It was called the Jesus Movement, or the Jesus People Movement. But that spiritual explosion did not originate at The University of California at Berkeley in Northern California. No, not at Berkeley. It started in Orange County, in Southern California.

When that spiritual explosion erupted in Orange County, it did not happen within Campus Crusade for Christ. We were back on the campuses wearing our button down collars, and trying to reach the establishment students, at fraternities and sororities, with the Gospel. When the Jesus Movement erupted, it began within the subculture, not on the campuses.

As mentioned above, I don't think any of us ever imagined that a big national impact would follow our witnessing on the Orange County beaches. But, the Lord said through Isaiah: **"So shall My word be that goeth forth out of My mouth: it shall not return unto Me void, but it shall accomplish that which I please, and it shall prosper in the thing whereto I sent it."** The Jesus Movement just seemed to explode when young people, many of them hippies and beach bums, trusted in Jesus. I am convinced that our sharing the Gospel, tens of thousands of times, during the preceding three summers prepared the way for that great spiritual harvest.

A group of Campus Crusade staff members, who returned to Berkeley about a year later, suggested that Campus Crusade needed a hippie division to minister to the subculture. It was decided that it would be better if it were an entirely separate organization, so there was a friendly "spin off." The group became known as the Christian World Liberation Front, or CWLF for short, and it published an outstanding Christian newspaper, directed to the radicals, called "Right On."

The Jesus People were very mobile and their movement spread like a wildfire.

Once it erupted, this movement spread like wildfire across the United States, Canada, and to other nations of the world.

Few in the hippie community had deep roots in one community. They were a very mobile people, and *as they were going*, thousands of longhaired hippies became evangelists, proclaiming the Good News wherever they wandered.

A few years later, Time Magazine traced the beginning of the Jesus People Movement to the ministry of Chuck Smith and Calvary Chapel in Costa Mesa, California. To their eternal credit, the believers at Calvary Chapel and the other evangelical churches of Orange County did a marvelous job of harvesting and nurturing the new converts.

Some older church people went through emotional trauma when their pews started to be filled by scraggly hippies and beach bums who called themselves "Jesus Freaks." But, most of the older believers in the Bible centered churches made the needed adjustment and accepted them.

The Jesus People Movement was a happening with no central human leadership. Rather, God raised up many men and women, independent of one another, who ministered to the subculture as the Lord directed them. Before long, there were Christian coffee houses and communes all over North America. I have to laugh when I look back on it now, as I remember that my attitude was not always the best when we went to those beaches. I now believe that God was doing at the beaches, what we were reading about in *The Principles of War* and trying to do at Berkeley and UCLA.

When the breakthrough happened, it had an impact on the whole battlefield, all over North America and even around the world -- just as was suggested in *The Principles of War*. The Jesus People in Southern California started pointing their fingers to the sky, symbolizing there is only "One Way" to get to heaven, and a popular bumper sticker appeared saying, "Honk if you love Jesus." Before long, these, and other visuals from the Jesus People Movement, were sweeping across the United States and Canada. Reports came back that Christian bumper stickers were even common in Europe.

As the movement gained momentum, straights (people who were not from the subculture) joined the parade. Many church youth groups rode the crest of the waves that, I believe, had its genesis on the beaches of Orange County, and many Christians all across America were encouraged to be bolder in their witness for Jesus.

It definitely made it easier for us to be effective witnesses on the campuses. There is no doubt that part of the phenomenal growth of the Campus Crusade ministry during those years can be traced back to the impact of the Jesus Movement on the youth of America.

To understand what a powerful impact the Jesus Movement had, consider the fact that Look, Time, and Newsweek magazines all had front-page covers that featured articles about the Jesus People. And, only five years after Time Magazine had that cover announcing that "God Is Dead," it named Jesus Christ as "The Man of the Year" for 1971.

Five years after Time Magazine had a cover that announced "God Is Dead," it named Jesus Christ as "The Man of the Year."

When the subculture declined in about 1973, many of the Jesus people were assimilated into evangelical churches around the world. While they may not want to admit it today, there are pastors in churches who began their spiritual journeys as long-haired, hippie Jesus Freaks. For sure, there are a lot of mature Jesus Freaks now sitting in the pews.

A few years ago, I talked to a professor from a Christian college who wrote his doctoral thesis on the Jesus Movement. He was taken aback when I told him about the tens of thousands of witnessing encounters that had taken place on the Orange County beaches during the summers before that spiritual explosion erupted. With a surprised look on his face, he said, "No one ever told me about that."

I also found another dissertation on the Jesus Movement on the Internet at www.ldolphins.ipindex.shtml (later the site was apparently discontinued). This dissertation was fascinating reading, was very well done, traces the background and history of the movement, and has extensive documentation. The author, Dave DiSabatino, apparently read nearly everything that had been written about the Jesus Movement, but apparently no one ever connected the dots and told him about the witnessing on the beaches.

Mr. DiSabatino wrote, "Many interpreters of this phenomena have offered various assessments of the Jesus People." And ... "Locating the genesis of any revival or spiritual movement is difficult. Unlike other North American revivals or awakenings that centered around one or two individuals, the Jesus People Movement had a number of beginnings through a number of different individuals."

"Although the origin of the Jesus People Movement has historically been linked to Southern California ... a number of missionaries began their work simultaneously without any previous knowledge of the others ... the best analysis of the origins of the movement is that it was a missionary invasion upon areas of counterculture. The overwhelming response to this impulse provided a spark which ignited the movement's blaze across the continent."

Mr. DiSabatino concludes in a summary paragraph, "The Jesus People Movement began in 1967 as a *spontaneous* missionary outreach by a handful of evangelically minded leaders to the counterculture." In response, I can't help but think, when a fire begins by *spontaneous* combustion, there has inevitably been something that preceded the explosion -- like a leaking pipe that filled a room with natural gas.

There are many valuable lessons from this historical happening. I believe that the tens of thousands of personal witnessing encounters that took place on those Orange County beaches during the three summers prior to the eruption of the Jesus Movement were like the gas that fills a room before a spark ignites the explosion. Yes, we need to pray for the Lord to visit us with a revival. But, we also need to work to create a spiritually explosive environment by consistently telling people the Good News about Jesus.

A common bit of advice that football coaches give to their players is that "When the going gets tough, the tough get going."

Let me reword that saying for Christians. "When the going gets tough, the witness for Jesus knows that God's Word will not return to Him void." Before the eruption of the Jesus People movement, it was a tough time for the evangelical church in America, and even tougher times may return. But, we need to always remember that we are on a winning team, because we work for a sovereign God!

There are signs today that the United States is in a spiritual free fall. But, I truly believe that any church or Christian organization that repeatedly saturates its area with the Gospel, like we saturated the beaches of Orange County, will ultimately see a mighty harvest. And, if millions of individual Christians will consistently tell others the Good News about Jesus, we can see spiritual awakenings even bigger than the Jesus Movement that began in the 60's. But, we each need to do our part!

If millions of Christians consistently tell others the Good News about Jesus, we can see a spiritual awakening bigger than the Jesus Movement.

Then there was Holy Hubert. God does not always send the kind of person we would select. I never would have thought of sending a "Holy Hubert" to a prestigious college like the University of California. But, as the Scriptures say, **"God chooses the foolish things of the world to confound the wise"** (I Corinthians 1:27). Romans 10:14 says, **"... how beautiful are the feet of those who bring the good news."** I did not check Hubert's feet, but I am sure they are beautiful.

There is also a lesson about follow up. I have heard some people suggest that we should not evangelize unless we can do proper follow up. Again, the Bible teaches that some plant, some water, but it is God who gives the increase. While I agree that we need to follow up new converts, I also know that the Holy Spirit of God is far more concerned with their spiritual needs than we are.

God is fully capable of leading new converts, who we can not follow up, to other Christians or to a fellowship of believers who will help them grow in their faith. It may not happen "tomorrow." But, the Scriptures say, **"Faithful is He who calls you, and He will also bring it to pass"** (2 Thessalonians 5:24). Yes, we need to follow up and disciple new believers, but we should never assume that we are the only members on God's team.

The overriding truth that I learned from the beaches of Orange County is the Scriptural principle that as you plant, so shall you reap (Galatians 6:7-8). We may not see instant results from our witnessing efforts, and we do not always see what God is doing. (In some cases, we may not find out until we get to heaven.) Our responsibility is to be obedient, and **"As we are going ... make disciples."** Those are the marching orders that Jesus gave us -- to *make disciples.*

By definition, a disciple is "a learner." We are commanded to help people learn about Jesus by sharing with them the truths from God's Word, the Bible. Our job is to tell others. It is the Holy Spirit's job to convict them of their need for Jesus. But, God gave us a precious promise in Isaiah when He said:

"My word will not return unto me void."

His Word, which we proclaimed "as we were going" to the beaches, did not return to Him void. God used it to "make disciples." I'm also confident that when I get to glory, I will meet disciples who came to know Jesus Christ as a result of our ministry at Berkeley. I pray that one of them will be that graduate student from Idaho.

Chapter Two

Prepare for Some Blessings

> Study to show thyself approved unto God, a workman that needeth not to be ashamed, rightly dividing the word of truth.
>
> II Timothy 2:15

There is an-often told story about a preacher who decided that he would not prepare his Sunday morning sermon. He decided that on Sunday morning, he would just walk to the pulpit, bow his head in prayer, and ask the Lord for a message.

During the following week, he did a lot of good things. He counseled with people who had problems. He met with his church staff, and he even performed a wedding. Sunday morning came, and he was ready with his prayer. When the time arrived for his sermon, he confidently walked up to the pulpit, bowed his head and silently prayed, "Lord, give me a message."

The Lord always answers our prayers, and he answered that preacher's prayer. He gave him a message. The message was, "You should have prepared!"

Many believers approach personal witnessing much like the preacher in this story. They just wing it, and hope that the Lord will give them the proper message. No doubt, sometimes the Holy Spirit will give a special message, and there are people who have come to know Christ as a result of such witnessing.

On the other hand, I truly believe that you will be much more effective if you take the time to prepare. You need to be ready with a definite plan of action for the witnessing opportunities that arise "as you are going" through life. I also believe that if you are prepared, God will know it, and will utilize your preparation. If you are not prepared, He may lead you away from those who are ready to become Christians, as He would not want you to bruise the ripe fruit.

Remember, the imperative in the Great Commission is to *make disciples.* A disciple is a learner, and as a witness for Jesus, you are a teacher. We would all be critical of a schoolteacher who did not prepare lesson plans. So also, a witness for Jesus is irresponsible if he/she does not have a teaching plan.

As a witnesses for Jesus, you have a big advantage over a preacher or a schoolteacher. You don't have to prepare a new sermon for every Sunday morning or a lesson plan for every class all year long. All you need is a few good messages that you can use many times.

You don't need a new message every week to be an effective witness. You do need a few messages that you can use over and over again.

While I have *been there and done that* as a minister with a congregation, in my personal witnessing I don't use a lot of messages. But, I have found that it is vital that I have about four well prepared ones. As we proceed in this book, I will share with you my primary witnessing messages. These messages were developed early in my Christian life, and I have been using them for many years.

The value of preparation was brought home to me late one afternoon at the University of Washington. As a staff member of Campus Crusade, I felt like I had the best job in the world. What a life! I was back in college, but did not have to go to class or take tests. And... I took a continual coffee break to talk to students about Jesus.

After a long day on campus, I was on my way out of the Student Union and heading back to a house our staff had rented near campus. As I passed the door to a coffee shop, I spotted a student sitting by himself. I said to the Lord, "I am too tired to do a random" (our term for witnessing when we did not have an appointment). But, I felt like the Lord wanted me to talk to this student, so I reluctantly walked over, asked him, "Can I join you?" and sat down.

There was a newspaper on the table, and as we chatted, I noticed a headline about the war in Vietnam. Using one of my favorite opening lines in that day, I commented, "Boy, that war in Vietnam is getting nasty." He agreed, and I continued on, "You just have to wonder whether the world will ever have any peace?" He commented that it was doubtful. I then said, "You know, I have found something that has helped me find peace as an individual. If you have a few minutes, I would like to share it with you. Do you have a few minutes?" He responded, "Sure, go ahead."

Before we continue on with this true story, let's analyze my approach. First, I used a current event as a stepping-stone to get into the Gospel. Until Jesus returns, you can count on there being a war, or turmoil, going on someplace in the world, and you can adapt this approach to the current conflict of the day. Second, I asked for permission to share with him. I have found that this is very helpful, and I follow this practice for several reasons: 1. It is polite, which is very important. 2. It gets a commitment to listen. 3. It reduces argumentation.

Ask permission before you share your faith:
It is the polite thing to do.
People are more likely to listen.
It usually reduces argumentation.

Back to the story. I was tired as a result of that daylong coffee break, and as I shared my message with this young man, I was holding a conversation with myself in my mind. It went something like this: "Bob, you are really blowing it. You are tired and you are doing a lousy job on this presentation of the Gospel. Why are you wasting your time? There is no way that anything will come from this when you are doing such a miserable job of telling him about Jesus."

As I was having this conversation with myself, I was continuing to go through my presentation just as I had several other times that day on my extended coffee break. But, I felt like mere words were coming out of my mouth, and that I was probably turning this student off of to anything spiritual.

As I got toward the end of my presentation of the Gospel, my internal conversation continued. I said to myself, "Bob, don't ask this student to pray to receive Christ. You don't deserve to have him accept the Lord when you have done such a poor job of presenting the Gospel."

But, again I felt a nudging from the Lord, so in obedience I wrote out an outline for a salvation prayer on the bottom of the sheet of paper I was using, and explained it to him. I then said, "Prayer is just talking to God. You don't have to get down on your knees, and you don't even have to close your eyes. You could make this prayer your prayer right now, and nobody else in this room will have any idea of what you are doing. Is there any reason that you would not like to pray and ask Jesus to be your Savior -- right now?"

To my surprise, he responded, "I would like to make that prayer my prayer." He bowed his head and prayed. When he completed his prayer, he looked up at me with a big smile on his face and excitedly said, "Boy, I can't wait to get home!" Somewhat taken aback, I asked, "What's the big hurry?" He responded, "My wife is a Christian, and she has been praying for me to become a Christian. But this is the first time that it has ever made sense to me, and I can't wait to get home and tell her what has happened." Needless to say, my jaw dropped a foot.

A few days later, I was moved to another campus, and I never got an opportunity to meet again with that student. But, I have no doubt that he did get adequate follow up, probably at his wife's church. I have no idea what has happened in his life. He is another whom I want to check on when I get to heaven.

This experience confirmed for me the value of preparation. I knew ahead of time what I wanted to share with him, and, in spite of being tired, the Lord used it. It also taught me not to depend on my emotions. I did not feel like I was communicating with him. For sure, I did not feel like I was "anointed" as I witnessed to him. But, the Holy Spirit was speaking to him, and the Lord never tires. As the psalmist said, "He never slumbers nor sleeps." (Psalm 121:4)

I was not the only instrument that the Lord used in that young husband's life, and not even the most significant one. After all, I am sure that his wife had spent far more time on her knees for him than I did in that single conversation. I am confident that my sharing the Gospel with him was God's response to her prayers.

It would have been fun to have become a little mouse and to observe his wife's response when he told her what happened that day on campus. It is likely that she called all of her friends the next day to tell them of how God had blessed her.

But, she was not the only one who received a blessing. I was tired when I sat down to share with him, but there was a spring in my step as I headed on home. One of the greatest blessings that God gives to believers is the privilege of being an instrument He uses to bring someone to Himself.

One of the great blessings that God gives to us is the privilege to be an instrument He uses to bring someone to Himself.

This young man also illustrates another important truth. Apparently, no one had ever before sat down with him and given him a clear explanation of the Gospel. It is my observation that, though we live in a nation where the Gospel message is readily available, it is still rare to find an unbeliever who understands the message of God's grace.

Very few non-Christians understand that, when Jesus died on the cross, He was our substitute who paid in full the penalty for our sin, and that God wants to give us the free gift of eternal life. Frankly, I have found that even many churchgoers mistakenly believe that they have to earn their standing with God.

I am sometimes critical of what often goes on under the name of evangelism. Sometimes it is an effort to get someone to "walk the aisle" in response to an emotional story when no biblical content has been communicated. Again, a disciple is a learner. To make disciples, we need to teach people who Jesus is and what He has done for them.

This was again brought home to me recently when I was in the maternity waiting room awaiting the delivery of my first grandchild. As I waited, I struck up a conversation with a young woman who was waiting for her friend to deliver. When I turned the conversation to spiritual questions, she told me that she had recently met some people who were believers, and that she and her husband had become new Christians with them. She assured me by saying, "Oh, I know about the rapture, and all of that."

But something did not seem quite right. As I probed further, I discovered that while she knew about the rapture, she had no understanding about Jesus dying on the cross as her substitute and for her sin. When I explained the Gospel to her, she got excited and was very thankful for what I shared with her.

Was this young lady already a Christian? Frankly, I don't know. But, I do know that she did not have a clear understanding of the Gospel truths. Maybe it had been presented to her and she did not comprehend it, or perhaps someone had failed to explain the most important information that should be communicated when making a disciple.

While the young man at the University of Washington and the young lady in the maternity waiting room were both excited by what they learned in our conversations, I also received blessings. One of the great joys in the Christian life comes when we share the good news about Jesus with others.

Both witnessing opportunities bore fruit because I was prepared -- ready to share my faith, "as I was going." The Lord is faithful, and, in both cases, He gave me the privilege of participating with them in their joy as they learned the good news about Jesus. So, be prepared. And, as you go, you too will receive some blessings as you help make disciples..

Chapter Three

Divine Appointments

He which soweth sparingly shall reap also sparingly; and he which soweth bountifully shall reap also bountifully.

II Corinthians 6:6

The year was 1970, and Campus Crusade for Christ had scheduled a training conference in personal evangelism to be held in October, at Ridgecrest, a Southern Baptist Conference center in North Carolina. I was in Houston at the time, and I encouraged a pastor, named John, to attend the conference.

John and his associate pastor decided to go to the conference to relax and enjoy the Appalachian Mountains as the leaves were changing their colors. Upon John's return to Houston, I stopped by to see him and asked him for his thoughts about the conference. John told me he really enjoyed the conference and then shared the following personal recollection:

"There were a couple of afternoons when we were sent out to practice what we were learning. When the first day of witnessing arrived, my associate pastor and I figured that we had already witnessed many times. So, instead of going out and witnessing, we rented a car, drove up and down the Blue Ridge Parkway, and enjoyed the beauty of autumn leaves in their blaze of multi-colored glory."

"Later that day there was a sharing time, and people told of the exciting witnessing experiences they had while we were enjoying our drive. As we sat there and listened, we felt like kicking ourselves and decided that on the next witnessing day, we would make up for the lost opportunity."

"A few days later we were sent out again. They suggested that we go door to door. But, we decided to go to a shopping center instead. We talked to a minister's wife, and a few other believers, but we did not find an opportunity to share our faith with any unbelievers, and frankly, I was a bit frustrated."

"Toward the end of the conference, I was standing outside on a veranda enjoying the natural beauty, and chatting with a man I had befriended earlier in the week. This new friend turned to me and asked, "Do you have one of those booklets they are using to tell people about Jesus?" I asked him, 'Didn't you get some when you registered for the conference?' He replied, 'Oh, I am not here for the conference. I work in the kitchen.'"

"I asked him if he was a Christian, and he responded, 'I don't think so.' I did not have a Four Spiritual Laws booklet with me so I said, 'Wait right here. I need to go to my room and get a booklet.' With the Four Spiritual Laws booklet in my hands, I quickly returned, and used it to explain the Gospel. The man responded and prayed to receive Jesus as his Savior".

"When he looked up after his prayer, he said to me, 'Let me tell you why I wanted to accept Christ today. Monday of this week, Dr. Bill Bright was walking through our kitchen. He got in a conversation with the head cook, talked to him about Jesus, and he became a Christian. His life has changed so much this week that I decided I wanted what he has.'"

Now we must ask, "What was Bill Bright doing in the kitchen leading the head cook to the Lord?" After all, as the president of Campus Crusade for Christ, he was a busy man. He was the main speaker at the conference, and I am sure there were a lot of very important people there who wanted to spend time with him. Ridgecrest is one of the largest Christian conference centers in the world, and hundreds of Christians, many of them preachers, had walked right by that cook without being sensitive to his need for Christ. So the question is, "How did Bill Bright happen to be in the kitchen talking to a cook, and how did he happen to be the one person sensitive to this man's need for the Savior?"

My first response to these questions is to reply, "I guess that's why God chose Bill Bright to be the leader of Campus Crusade for Christ." Apparently, the other believers who walked by the head cook were not sensitive to the fact that he did not know Christ as Savior. Again the question is, "Why was Bill the one whom God used to reach this man with the Gospel?"

Having heard Bill share his heart with the staff many times, I think I know why he was the one God used. Bill practices what he preaches. One thing that he preaches is that we need to be sensitive to "divine appointments." I have heard him say many times, "Every day, I ask God to make me aware of divine appointments." Anytime Bill Bright is alone with someone, he asks himself, "Is this a divine appointment to tell this person about Jesus?"

We need to ask God to make us aware of the Divine Appointments that He sets for us.

During my last year in seminary, I was an associate staff member of Campus Crusade. Bill Bright came to Portland, and I had the privilege of driving him to a speaking engagement. On our way back after the meeting, we stopped at a Dairy Queen. Bill suggested that we thank the Lord for our ice cream cones. When we bowed our heads, the girl behind the counter asked if something was wrong. I started to say no, and, with a tender voice, Bill said to her, "We were just thanking the Lord for our ice cream. *Do you know Jesus as your Savior?*" I don't recall the girl's response, but I do remember that it was an important lesson for a young seminarian.

I was not at the IBS (Institute of Biblical Studies) that Campus Crusade for Christ held at Cornell University one summer in the late sixties. But later in the summer, when I arrived at Arrowhead Springs, everyone who had been at Cornell was talking about something that had happened while Bill Bright was speaking.

Dr. Bright had stopped by the IBS for a few days to deliver his messages on the Holy Spirit, and these special sessions were opened to students who were attending summer school. This was during the Vietnam conflict, campuses across America were in turmoil, and student anti-war protests were common.

Dr. Bright's last message was on how to love by faith. Near the end of his message, a Cornell student rose to his feet in the back of the room and yelled, "Dr. Bright, I have a question."

Bill responded by asking the student what he wanted to know. The student sarcastically yelled back, "Have you ever given this message to the Pentagon?" Bill politely responded, "No, I have not. But if I am ever given the opportunity, I would be pleased to do so." To Bill's answer, the student responded in a loud voice, "If you have not given this message to the Pentagon, then I think you are half of a Christian."

With a meek and mild spirit, Bill asked the student, "Young man, are you a Christian?" The student responded by saying, "Well, not by your definition of Christianity." Again, with a sweet spirit, Bill said, "Then I need to talk to you about Jesus. Would you come down here right now so I can tell you about Jesus?" As the young man meekly walked forward, Bill dismissed the meeting so he could share the Gospel with the young protester. The next day, that young man accepted Jesus Christ as his Savior.

When that young man tried to insult him, Bill Bright was not concerned with protecting his personal honor. But, he was deeply concerned about this young man's need to know Jesus as his Savior. I am confident that he was also silently praying, "God, is this a divine appointment that you have set for me?"

"... Look on the fields; for they are white already to harvest." Jesus (John 4:35).

We can all learn from Dr. Bill Bright's example. The opportunities to witness for Jesus are abundant. So remember, whenever you are going, wherever you are going, and for whatever reason you are going, ask God to make you sensitive to the divine appointments He gives you. If you do, and if you are prepared to clearly present the Gospel, you can count on Him to give you opportunities so that *"As you are going..."* you will *"make disciples."*

Chapter Four

Whoever Asks the Questions

Walk in wisdom toward them that are without, redeeming the time. Let your speech be always with grace, seasoned with salt, that ye may know how to answer every man.
Colossians 4:5-6

People often comment, "You should never mix religion and politics." Personally, they are my two favorite subjects of conversation, and I love to mix them. Furthermore, I have found that politics and current events can serve as great launching pads to share the Gospel with unbelievers.

Several years ago, when I lived in College Station, Texas, I attended a community meeting sponsored by our Congressman in the U.S. House of Representatives. Among the groups who attended and wanted to espouse their particular agenda, there was a group of six students from Texas A&M whom you could describe as "the gay delegation."

After the meeting was concluded, numerous people hung around and discussed issues. As I was about to leave, I could not help but overhear a heated argument between a gentleman and the gay delegation. He was accusing them of spreading AIDS, and they were arguing that AIDS was not a disease spread solely by homosexuals.

After listening for a few minutes, I decided that this might be a divine appointment. So I asked, "May I ask you guys some questions?" They said, "Sure!" The gentleman who had been arguing with them used my question as an excuse for a fast exit.

I started by commenting, "Let me first say, I personally think that homosexual behavior is wrong, but I don't think that it is any worse than adultery." They all quickly agreed. (I mentally noted that this was an admission that their homosexual behavior was wrong, but ignored that because I did not want to waste my time on that issue. I had another goal in mind.)

I continued on, "Now, I'm like Will Rogers; I only know what I read in the newspapers. But, what I read is that the initial spread of AIDS in America was because of promiscuous behavior by homosexuals. I've read that many homosexuals would have several hundred sex partners in a single year. Is that true?" One of them responded, "That kind of stuff used to happen, but we have learned our lesson and it does not happen any more!" I responded, "I'm sure glad that you have stopped that."

Then I asked, "Well, what would happen if someone came along with a cure for AIDS and wiped it off of the face of the globe? Isn't it likely that homosexuals would return to their former promiscuous behavior?" One member of the delegation quickly responded, "No, we have learned our lesson!" A friend standing next to him, looked at him in unbelief and said, "Who are you trying to kid? You know we would." I have to admit, I had to fight back the inclination to laugh.

I continued on, "Let me ask another question. I'm sure you have heard of something called the Ten Commandments. Why do you think they were given, and what was their purpose?" One of them responded, "I guess it was a moral code that someone suggested people should follow."

When someone says:
"I have not done anything wrong."
The law shouts: "Oh, Shut up!"

To his answer, I responded, "Would you believe that according to the Bible, that is almost the opposite of their purpose?" One of them asked, "What do you mean by that?" I said, "Well, the books of Romans and Galatians explain that the Law was given to shut their mouth. Let me explain how: When someone says, 'I haven't done anything wrong,' the Bible responds, 'Let's take a look at the Law.' In essence the Law shouts back, **'Oh, shut up!'** You could say that the Ten

Commandments were meant to be diagnostic, to help us understand our problems."

They all chuckled a bit and, before they could comment further, I continued on, "Let me ask you guys another question. Let's assume that as you are heading back to campus, a ten-ton truck hits you, you are all killed, they pull the curtain, and your show is over. What do you think would happen to you and why? Do you believe in a life after death? Do you believe in a heaven and a hell?" And I repeated, "What do you think would happen to you and why?"

Before any of them could answer, I turned to the student on my far right, pointed to him and asked, "How would you answer that question?" He quickly answered, "I am an atheist. I don't believe in a life after death. I just believe that when I die, my life will end, and that's all there is to it." Without commenting on his answer, I quickly turned to the next student and asked, "How would you answer the question?" Before he could answer, one of the other students interrupted and asked, "How would you answer that question?" And, then all of the others chimed in, "Yea! How would you answer your own question?"

I quickly responded, "Look, I will give you my answer, but I need to hear all of yours first. But, I promise you I will give you my answer. Is that O.K.?" They all agreed, and I repeated my question to the second student. I don't recall the answers from the second through fourth students, but as they were answering, the student on the left end was nervously pacing the floor. Finally, it was his turn, and I pointed his way and asked, "How would you answer the question?"

He nervously answered, "Well, I'm a Roman Catholic and I know how they feel about homosexuality, but I don't agree with them." I interrupted him and said, "They would say it is a mortal sin. Right?" He agreed, but he insisted that he did not think he had done anything so bad that he would go to hell. Again, I did not challenge his wrong answer. I knew what would follow, and I kept my objective in mind.

Having all given their answers, they turned to me and again insisted that I give my answer. So I said, "Look, I'll give you my answer, but for it to make any sense, there are some things I need to explain first. Without this explanation, my answer won't register with you. It will just take a few minutes, and then I can give my answer. Is that O.K?" They agreed, and I proceeded to give them my regular Gospel presentation. (See chapter six.)

After explaining the Gospel to them, I said, "Now for my answer to the question. I know that I would go to be with God. Not because I am a good guy, or any better than anyone else, or any better than any of you. But, because Jesus paid in full the price for my sin when He died on the cross, and that God has forgiven me." There were a few friendly closing comments, which I don't recall, and we headed to our respective cars to leave.

When God gives you a divine appointment, be sure you keep your objective in mind.

Let's review this happening and analyze what I was doing, and why:

First, from the beginning of the conversation to the end, I had one goal in mind. I wanted the opportunity to explain the Gospel to make sure that each one of them understood what Jesus did for them on the cross. When we parted, I knew that I had accomplished that objective. I had planted some seeds.

Second, I clearly let them know that I did not think that God approved of their sin. But I was careful to avoid having a self-righteous attitude. A self-righteous, or "look down your nose," attitude can instantly turn people off and close their ears.

Third, I accomplished this goal by asking questions. My objective was to gain permission to present the Gospel. To reach that objective I asked a series of questions. Always remember, the person who is asking the questions is the one who controls the direction of the conversation.

Finally, I did not sense that any of them were ready to accept Christ, and did not feel that it was the appropriate time or place to ask them to pray and to receive Christ. But,

I am confident that seeds were planted and that the Lord can move other believers to water and fertilize them.

The person who asks the right questions is the one who determines the direction of a conversation.

The Great Commission commands us to make disciples (plural) as we are going. It is my observation that it is rare when someone comes to know Christ because of the influence of only one person. Frankly, I can't recall one person who has come to know Christ solely as a result of my witness. This may not be true for missionaries in remote parts of the world. But in America, you can almost count on it that people have been exposed to the Gospel before you witness to them.

When someone comes to know Christ, it is usually the result of a process wherein several people have shared with him or her before they finally make the decision to accept Jesus. The process is some plant, some water, some fertilize, some may even prune, and finally, God gives the increase. (A paraphrase of I Corinthians 3:6.) This implies to me that we all need to share Christ with a lot of people. Do not get discouraged when someone does not respond to your witness -- it may turn out that you have contributed to a future decision for Jesus Christ.

The process is some plant, some water, some fertilize, some may even prune, and finally, God gives the increase.

Friendship evangelism is a popular concept in the church today. Using this plan, believers are encouraged to establish relationships with non-believers, win the right to be heard by being a friend, and then, when the right time arrives, share the Gospel. I am sure there are people who have come to know Jesus as Savior as a result of implementing this strategy, and I am thankful for them. But, for many believers, the hardest people to witness to are the people they know the best, and the toughest of all are their close relatives.

I have met believers who have come to know Christ because they saw something different in a believer's life and wanted it (just like the cook in the previous chapter). But, I have met far more who came to know Jesus because of what they saw in Him. I personally believe that the concept that we must first win the right to be heard (by the quality of our own lives) is a misconception.

When I was in seminary, I would occasionally study late at night in a coffee shop. I usually sat at a counter, and from time to time I would get into a conversation with someone and try to share my faith.

Late one night, a gentleman sat down next to me whose appearance indicated to me that he might be a refugee from the local skid row. We struck up a conversation, and my observation turned out to be correct. When I made a transition in the conversation to share the Gospel with him, I got a big surprise. It turned out that this gentleman had come to know Jesus as his Savior at a rescue mission.

As we chatted, he readily admitted to me that he did not yet have the victory over alcohol. But, he proceeded to tell me how much he enjoyed witnessing to the other men he met on the streets. After listening to him for a while, I could not help but remember a definition I had heard for a Christian witness; "A witness for Jesus is one beggar telling another beggar where he found a soft touch."

"A witness for Jesus is one beggar telling another beggar where he found a soft touch."

There is an inherent danger when trying to win the right to be heard by your life style. It is all too easy to come off as being self-righteous. A proper attitude should be, "I am a sinner saved by His grace, I'm no better than you, but I am forgiven because of what Jesus did for me when He died on the cross.

And ... He will forgive you, too, if you just place your faith in Him as your Savior." That was the attitude I tried to have with the gay delegation, and there was never any hostility in our discussion. Before we parted, a couple of them even commented that they had enjoyed meeting and talking with me.

Frankly, I am sure that my friend from the streets of Portland was far more effective in witnessing to his buddies than I could have ever been. He wasn't trying to convince them that he was a good person, but he was excited about telling them how God had forgiven him and how they could also be forgiven and inherit eternal life through believing in Jesus.

I am not opposed to making friends so that you can share your faith. I think it is a great idea. But remember, the longer you wait, the harder it may be for you to effectively share your faith with them.

Furthermore, most of us are only capable of having a very limited number of close friendships during any extended period of time. To be obedient to Christ's instructions in the Great Commission and make disciples "as we are going," we need to be sensitive to every opportunity, and not merely make a few friends so that we can witness to them. If you are available "as you are going" in your day-by-day activities, God will often give you divine appointments when you least suspect them.

Learn how to ask the right questions!

In my experience, I have found that the easiest way for me to find out whether I am on a divine appointment when I meet a new person is though the effective use of questions. When I meet someone and we are able to have a private conversation, I try to show an interest in them and ask them questions about themselves. Most people love to talk about themselves and when they find a willing listener, they will often open up.

After listening for a while, I like to ask my favorite questions, the questions I asked each of the gay students in the story at the beginning of this chapter. If you have ever taken the course called Evangelism Explosion, offered by James Kennedy and the people at Coral Ridge Presbyterian Church in Florida, you will recognize these questions.

I usually preface my question by saying, "I have a question I would like to ask you. I have asked it of a lot of people in my lifetime, and it is always interesting to hear different people's answers to this question." I then embellish the Evangelism Explosion question like this. "Now, I would not want this to happen, but, if as you are driving home tonight, you are hit by a ten ton truck, they pull the curtain and your show is over. What do you think would happen to you and why?" Then I continue, "Do you believe in a heaven and hell? Do you believe in a life after death? What do you think would happen to you, and WHY?"

Listen for their WHY, rather than their WHERE.

When I ask these questions, I am not concerned about where they think they would go. What I really want to know is their answer to WHY.

If additional prompting is needed, I often say, "I have asked that question of a lot of people. Some people think that when their final curtain is pulled and the show is over, that's it. Some people think they would go to hell. Some think they would go to heaven, and others just answer, "I don't have the least idea." I pause and continue on; "Let's say you finally knock on the proverbial pearly gates, and the Lord asks you, 'Why should I let you in here?' How would you answer?"

The goal in asking these questions is to find out, as well as I can, whether the person knows Jesus as their Savior. The key is their answer to WHY. My experience is that those who think they will go to heaven focus their answer in one of two different directions:

Some focus on what they personally have or have not done. They usually frame their answer, "Well, I have not done that much that is bad," or "I have tried to be a good person." (These wrong answers indicate that they probably don't know Jesus as their Savior). Others focus on what Jesus did for them on the cross (the right answer -- they probably do know Jesus).

There is a third group we used to call Lady Clairol Christians; "Only the Lord knows for sure!" (A take off on an old TV commercial; "Only your hairdresser will know for sure.") They allude to having faith, but they are often hard to pin down.

I never get into an argument or criticize someone's response to these questions, and I try to avoid being judgmental. My purpose in asking it is to find out whether they know Christ, not to open up an argument.

Sometimes I leave the spiritual subject and continue to ask them other questions about themselves before popping the most important question of all. But, I always keep my goal in mind. I want to get permission to share the Gospel. Again, I can't overemphasize that, at this time, I ignore any negatives.

The big question is, "If you have a few minutes, I would like to share with you the most important thing I have ever learned in my lifetime. May I share it with you?" When I put it that way, many (not all) warmly grant me a hearing.

The big question is, "If you have a few minutes, I would like to share with you the most important thing I have ever learned in my lifetime. May I share it with you?"

Again, as mentioned in chapter two, there are three important reasons that you should ask for permission before you share the gospel. First, it is polite. Second, if they give you permission they are more likely to listen. Third, it creates an atmosphere that reduces argumentation (not asking permission can make people defensive). If you knock first, people are more likely to graciously open their mental doors.

Once they have given you permission, you have a great opportunity to use some of your time "as you are going ... to Make a Disciple."

Using a military analogy, to have a great Spiritual awakening, we need "troops on the ground" getting into many conversations about the Gospel with unbelievers. When you came to know Jesus as your Savior, God drafted you to be a foot soldier for Jesus. His marching orders are, "As you are going ... Make Disciples." Ask questions and you won't be an inductee who is missing in action.

Chapter Five

A Sword is a Sword is a Sword

For the word of God is quick and powerful, and sharper than any two edged sword, piercing even to the dividing asunder of soul and spirit, and of the joints and marrow, and is a discerner of the thoughts and intents of the heart.
Hebrews 4:12

As a general rule, Campus Crusade for Christ has the female staff members meet evangelistically with the coeds and the men meet with the male students. But, when I started the ministry at Western Washington University, in the winter of 1966, I was the only Campus Crusade staff member ministering on the campus. Consequently, if one of our Christian students needed help, I would occasionally help in witnessing to a coed.

One of the coeds active in our group asked me to meet with her and a friend from her dorm, because she had some tough questions and objections to the Gospel. We met in the coffee shop at the Student Union. (Some of our Christian students thought it was my office.)

After explaining the Gospel, answering some questions, and sharing some Christian evidences with this young woman, something happened that has never happened to me before or since. She started to cry, jumped up from her chair, and almost ran out of the coffee shop.

After making a few suggestions to the Christian student on how to handle the matter, I spotted some of our Christian male students across the coffee shop trying to witness to another student. I walked over and joined them, and quickly discovered that the unbeliever loved to debate (I later found out he was a member of the debate team). Frankly, he was having fun shooting down the students who were trying to witness to him. They couldn't get a word in edgewise before he would object to what they said, and then he would ask another question.

After sizing him up for a few minutes, I interrupted the conversation and said to him, "You and I need to get together tomorrow for an appointment." He looked at me somewhat surprised and asked, "What for?" Confident that he would rise to a challenge, I said to him, "For just one purpose, to convert you." With a smirk on his face, he said, "This sounds like fun." So, we set a time.

The next day, I had quite a surprise. Right off the bat, he said, "Well, I hear you are a professional evangelist," and he let me know that the student who had run out of the room the day before was his girl friend. He implied that she had "filled him in on me," and warned him to "watch out." The tone of his voice told me that he was geared up for an all out verbal war.

I responded that I had never been given that title before, but I was not offended. I asked him a few questions about himself and made a transition by asking him if I could share the Four Spiritual Laws with him. He said O.K., and I proceeded.

After making a few comments about Law One, *"God loves you and has a wonderful plan for your life,"* I started to go to the second law, and he almost jumped up and down saying, "You can't go to your second point. You have not proved your first point yet. You can't go to your second point until you have proved your first premise. You have to prove it to me!"

I instantly realized that I was not going to get anyplace with this student using my normal approach, so I said something I had never said before, and I have never felt led to use since. With indignation, I responded, "Buddy, who do you think you are to tell me how I should present my message to you? Let's get one thing straight. I am not trying to prove that what the Bible says is true. Socrates said, 'define your terms.' That is all I am doing, defining terms so we are both talking about the same thing. And, I would prefer to explain my message to you my way, and not yours. Then, after I have explained to you what the Bible says, you can object all you want. Is that O.K.?" With a surprised look on his face, he said, "Well, O.K.," and I went forward with my explanation of the Gospel.

By the time I finished explaining the Gospel, his attitude had dramatically changed, and I was able to share with him some Christian evidences "to see if this message is true." (We will discuss some of the evidences later in this book.)

At the end of our conversation, he apologized and said, "I must admit that I had a chip on my shoulder when we started talking. But, I realize now that I did not understand the message of the Bible. And, I have to admit, I never realized that there was this kind of evidence for Christianity." Then he added, "I have a lot of thinking to do."

This student was not ready to trust in Jesus as his Savior and, he had not accepted Christ before Campus Crusade moved me to North Carolina. I want to check on both him and his girl friend when I get to heaven. I am confident that both understood "the way" after our conversations.

Never argue about the inspiration of the Bible, or try to defend it, until you have first explained the salvation message in the Bible.

I share this story, not to suggest that you should use the tactic I used with him. Rather, I share it because it illustrates an important principle. Never argue about the inspiration of the Bible, or try to defend it, until you have first explained the salvation message in the Bible.

A lot of Christians think that they must first establish that the Bible is the inspired word of God before someone will believe its message. But, the Bible explains that it is a super sharp, two-edged sword. (Hebrews 4:12)

Think about it. If you are going into battle with a sword in your hand, do you have to first prove to the enemy that it is actually a sword? No! It would be silly to hold a debate with the enemy to establish that the piece of shiny steel in your hand is a sword. If the enemy adamantly denies that it is a sword, a thrust into his body will still cut. Don't worry about proving that the Bible is a sword. Just use it!

It is important that you always keep your objective in mind. When I sat down with this antagonistic debater, I knew that he did not understand the truths of the Gospel. I had one main goal in mind, to get the privilege of sharing the biblical truths about Jesus with him. I was not about to get in a debate with him when he had no understanding of the Gospel.

To be an effective witness -- stay on message

When you listen to the political commentators discuss a candidate for a political office, it is often said that he is either a strong or weak candidate based on whether he is able to "stay on message." The same principle applies to us as witnesses for Jesus Christ. Some people will bring up questions or objections that can easily get us off of our message. A good way to *stay on message* is to say, "That's a good question. You will be able to better understand my answer to that question if you will let me first finish this explanation of the Bible's message. We will come back to it later. Is that O.K.?"

Once the Gospel is properly explained, it will answer many questions and eliminate most of the objections. Experience has taught me that very few people, who have objections to the Gospel, actually have a clear understanding of the message of God's grace. It is vital that we keep that in mind and focus our efforts on getting the opportunity to give them a clear explanation of the Gospel. So, stay on your message!

There are only two issues about the Bible that I ever deal with before presenting the message of God's grace. Some people try to say that the Bible has been translated so many times that it cannot be trusted, and others will challenge the authenticity of the documents because they were written so long ago. Both are easy to quickly answer.

In response to the translation issue, I say, "The more translations we have the better! The good news is that we are not dependent on one person's translation. When we compare the many translations, by different people of a variety of theological persuasions, they may use slightly different wordings, but there are no significant differences in meanings."

"But, if you are really concerned, you can get Hebrew and Greek grammars and lexicons and translate it yourself. But I must warn you. If you publish your translation, and it has any errors, there are thousands of experts in Hebrew and Greek who will be quick to point out your mistakes."

Many skeptics challenge the transmission of the original texts. They usually object by saying, "It is a very old book. How can we know for sure that we have what it actually said?" I respond by quickly drawing a simple diagram on a sheet of paper -- about like the following:

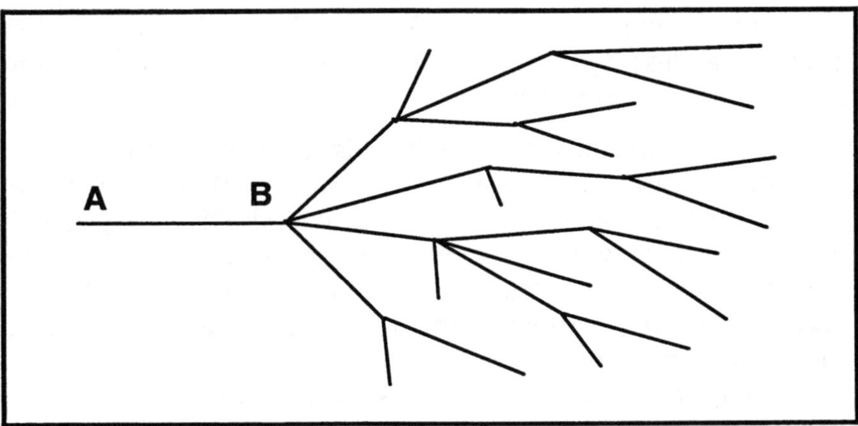

As I draw it, I explain, "As an example, Paul wrote a letter from Rome (point A) to Ephesus (point B). At Ephesus it was copied by hand and the copies were sent to other cities such as Thessalonica, Galatia, Antioch, and Jerusalem. In each of these locations, they made more copies and sent them on to others.

You could say that copies sprang forth like the branches on a tree. There were thousands of "branches!" But remember:

1. **There were no printing presses in those days.**
2. **Each copy was made by hand, and passed on to others.**
3. **It would have been impossible to retrieve and change all of the scattered copies.**
4. **There are more fragments of the Bible's text than from any other writings from antiquity.**

5. All the variant reading in the various New Testament texts could be condensed to one page of a Greek New Testament.

6. The variant readings are minor and do not affect any major teaching in the Bible. (Often it's just a single letter in a word.)

"True, we don't have the original that was sent from Rome to Ephesus. But, thank God! If we had it, every fool in the world would want to take a pilgrimage to worship it. When all of the copies of the biblical documents are compared, one with another, there is no doubt that we have the essence of the messages that were in the original documents."

It has been rare that I have had anyone continue to object after using these two simple explanations. Feel free to use them and make them your own.

In the church world, there is a big debate over the issue of biblical inerrancy. While I believe strongly that the original texts of the Bible were inerrant, this is a debate that I avoid with unbelievers for several reasons: First, it puts me on the defense, and as often noted, "the best defense is a good offense." Second, it often becomes a smoke screen that is used to avoid the more important issues (for an unbeliever) of who Jesus is, and what He accomplished for us on the cross. Finally, one does not need to believe in the inerrancy of the Scriptures to become a Christian. If an unbeliever brings up the subject, I merely say, "There are differing views on that issue among sincere Christians, and there are more important questions for us to explore." Then I move on.

Some people will question whether the Bible is actually a revelation from God, or they will assert that they believe the Bible is "just another book written by men." I don't argue the issue. Instead of arguing, I silently remind myself that a sword is a sword is a sword, and then tenderly use it as a sword.

Always remember, you don't have to prove the Bible is a sword. The Holy Spirit can use God's Word, to cut to the quick, even if someone does not believe that it is a sword.

"As you are going..." remember, the Bible
is a super sharp sword that you can
use to *"Make Disciples."*

Chapter Six

Show and Tell Time

And the things which you have heard from me in the presence of many witnesses, these entrust to faithful men who will be able to teach others also.

II Timothy 2:2

One Sunday evening after church, a group of us from the college-career group at the First Baptist Church in Salem, Oregon decided to relax and have some fellowship at a local restaurant. As we entered the restaurant, one member of our group greeted a friend, who happened to walk in at the same time, and suggested that he join us.

As we fellowshipped together, one of the members of our group made a comment about the church service, and our new friend made a sarcastic comment about Christianity. No one knew quite how to respond. I waited until everyone was ready to leave, and asked him if I could ask him some questions. He replied "Sure," and we stayed at the table as the rest of the group departed.

As we chatted, I learned that he was a philosophy major who assumed that religion was a waste of time. I asked for permission to "share something" with him that had "really helped me," and he consented.

During my explanation of the Gospel, I made the statement that "God is absolutely holy, righteous, and pure." He instantly interrupted and said, "There is no such thing as an absolute!" I quickly responded by asking him, "Are you absolutely sure of that?" He had to laugh at himself, as his objection was an obvious contradiction of terms.

Knowing that one of the popular philosophical practices was linguistic analysis, I said, "Let's assume that pluses represent good things and minuses represent bad things or anything short of perfection. God being absolutely holy and pure is all pluses, and no minuses at all." As I explained this, I put some pluses above the words Holy God, on the diagram I had just scribbled on a piece of paper. He said, "O.K., we can use that as a definition." (This diagram is found later in this chapter.)

I then said, "There is no doubt that every man has some minuses." As I spoke, I put some minuses under the words "sinful man" on my diagram. I continued by asking him, "What would happen if God, who is all pluses, overlooked a man's minuses, and allowed that man to come into fellowship with Himself?" He looked at my diagram, thought for a few seconds, and responded, "That would be a minus and God would no longer be all pluses." I, of course, agreed with his conclusion.

Several weeks before this conversation, I had heard a pair of messages on a Sunday morning and evening that were given by Dr. Arthur B. Whiting, my English Bible professor in Seminary. In the morning, his sermon title was, "Some things that God cannot do." In the evening his message was titled, "More things that God cannot do."

These messages were expositions of verses in the Bible that assert things that God cannot do, such as "God, who cannot lie" (Titus 1:2), "He cannot deny Himself" (James 1:13), "God cannot be tempted by evil" (James 1:13), "He could swear by no one greater (than Himself)" (Hebrews 6:13), and "Thine eyes are too pure to approve evil, and Thou canst not look on wickedness with favor" (Habakkuk 1:13).

By combining the response the Holy Spirit gave to me when the philosophy student said, "There is no such a thing as an absolute" and what I learned from Dr. Whiting's sermons, I came up with a teaching that I have repeatedly used in my witnessing presentations for over thirty years. I have found it is effective, and please feel free to "borrow it" and use it.

As I share the Gospel, I always tell about talking to that philosophy student, and his response to my statement that

"God is absolutely holy, and righteous," my comeback, and an explanation of the truth he uncovered, that there are some things that God cannot do.

Sometimes, I add some additional humor by inserting, "This guy was about like the philosophy student who came home from college and his mother asked him, 'How are you, son?' He responded, 'Relative to what?'" (I have learned that a little bit of *entertainment* here and there in a presentation helps hold their attention, and this joke illustrates the biblical teaching about the foolishness of philosophy.)

Our popular American culture has no absolutes.

We live in a time when popular culture asserts that there are no absolutes, and there does not seem to be much concern over the possibility of facing a judgment after death with eternal consequences. We have a lot of what I call *practical atheists.* They say they believe in God, but they think and live like atheists. The Epicureans of ancient Rome who advocated, "Eat, drink, and be merry, for tomorrow we die," had nothing on our generation in America.

We must confront people with God's holiness.

I believe it is important that we confront people with God's holiness. In light of this, I tell about the conversation with that philosophy student to add, what I believe, is an important fourth point to the common three point salvation message, or a fifth point to a four point message like the Four Spiritual Laws.

A short version of a typical three-point Gospel message is 1. Man is sinful, 2. Jesus paid the price for our sin, and 3. You must place your faith in Jesus as your Savior to get to heaven. The Four Spiritual laws starts with a positive additional point, that God loves you.

For many, starting on the positive is helpful. Though I was on the Campus Crusade staff for many years and greatly respect that organization, in my typical explanation of the Gospel, I usually bypass the positive start and begin with the problem created by our sin. (Though I still use some of the diagrams from the Four Spiritual Laws booklet.) A summary of my four-point outline is:

1. Man is sinful and thus separated from God.
2. God is Holy and He cannot overlook your sin.
3. Jesus Christ's death on the cross is God's loving provision for your sin.
4. You must place your faith in Jesus as your Savior

Before I get to my third point, God's solution for man's sin problem, I want to make sure that they understand that God can't merely overlook their sin, that God's holiness demands absolute moral purity. When confronted with this truth, a student at the University of Washington responded, "Good night! We're sunk! What are we going to do?"

That student did not give that response to me. His was a response to a witness by Robert Andrews, a fellow Campus Crusade for Christ staff member. Notice that I used his statement without saying that he said it to me. This illustrates how you can "borrow" illustrations and yet remain honest.

Applying this principle, you can use my illustration about the philosophy student without saying that he said to you that there is no such thing as an absolute. For example, you could word it, "When a philosophy student was told that God is absolutely holy, righteous, and pure, he responded, 'There is no such a thing as an absolute." Of course, the obvious question was, "Are you absolutely sure of that? He was absolutely sure that there are no absolutes." Or, you can preface it by saying "Someone shared with a philosophy student that..."

Preachers "borrow" illustrations from each other every day, and you can too. As Solomon put it, **"There is nothing new under the sun."** But, I think it is important that you not misrepresent an illustration as being personal when you are sharing the Gospel. In the sample Gospel presentation that follows, I will use this illustration in another way you can copy.

The remainder of this chapter is my person-to-person presentation of the Gospel. (Please understand, I don't claim my way is the only way, or even the best way, to present the Gospel.) I will editorialize in italics along the way. The regular print is what I say as I witness. (Some quotation marks are eliminated.)

I like to start witnessing with a blank sheet of paper in front of us with the other person on my right, so he can watch as I write. (As mentioned in chapter one, a paper napkin in a coffee shop is often a handy alternative to a sheet of paper.) I start by drawing two lines at the top of the paper, and write Holy God above the top line and Sinful Man under the bottom line, and then say, "The bible explains that God is absolutely holy, righteous and pure, and man is sinful." *My diagram then looks about like this:*

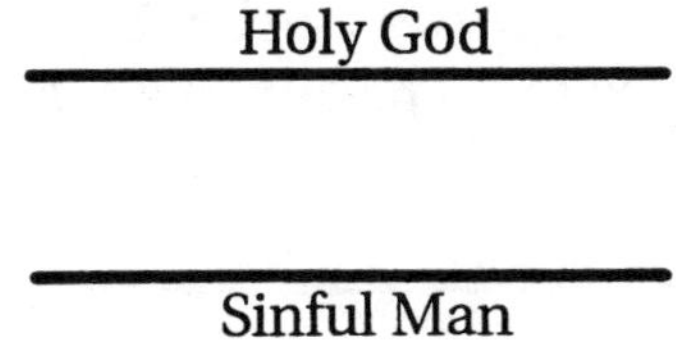

Throughout history, men have tried to pierce through the barrier that was created by our sin. Some have tried through religion, others through philosophy, and still others through trying to live a moral and ethical life. *I draw three arrows going up from the bottom line and write R, P, and E next to the arrows as I use the three words they represent.*

But, there is a problem. Romans 3:23 says, "All have sinned and fall short of the glory of God." And Romans 6:23 says, "The wages of sin is death." Consequently our sin blocks our fellowship with God!

As I say this I write, "Romans 3:23" and under it, "All have sinned." A little lower on the page I write, "Romans 6:23" and under it, "Wages = Death."

I continue on: "No matter how hard we try through religion, philosophy or just trying to live a good life, we are still in the category of the ALL who have SINNED, and the PAYMENT for our sin is DEATH." *As I say this, I underline* **"All have sinned" and "Wages = DEATH"** *on the sheet of paper.*

Continuing on: But, let's take another look at this. When a college student, who was a philosophy major, looked at this drawing and was told that "God is absolutely holy, righteous, and pure" *(an important word to communicate the truth),* he immediately responded, "There is no such thing as an absolute!" Of course, the logical response to his assertion was, "Are you absolutely sure of that?" *Most people chuckle at this point.*

This student studied linguistic analysis, so it was explained, "Let's say that pluses represent good things and minuses represent bad things, or anything short of perfection. Since God is absolutely holy, righteous, and pure, He is all pluses and no minuses at all. *As I say this, I put a string of pluses above Holy God.* But, there is no doubt that man has minuses. *I put some minuses under Sinful Man as I say this. My sheet of paper now looks about like this:*

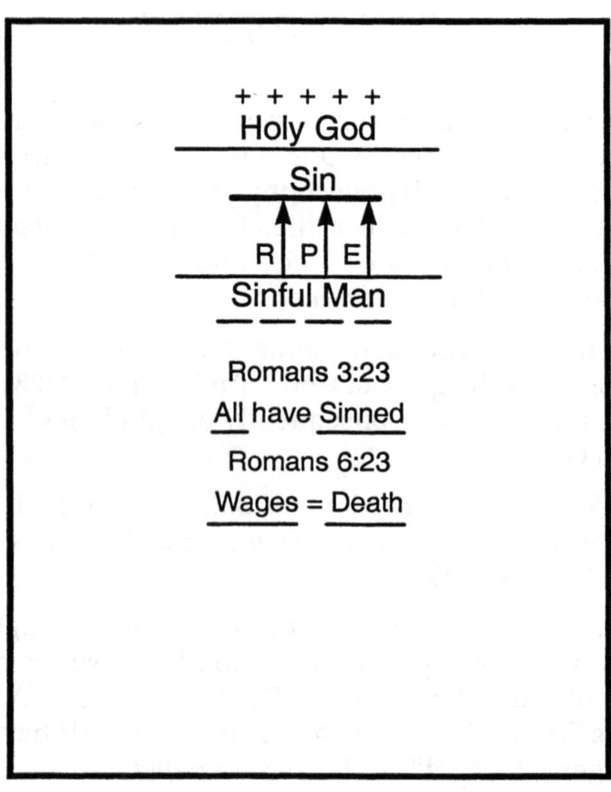

The student replied, "We can use that as a definition." He was then asked, "What would happen if God, who is absolutely holy, righteous, and pure, merely overlooked our sin (our minuses), and He allowed us to come into fellowship with Himself?" The philosophy student took a second look at the diagram and responded, "If God were to overlook even one minus, that would be a minus, and God would no longer be all pluses."

That philosophy student had come to understand an important teaching in the Bible, that there are some things God cannot do. For example, the Bible tells us "God cannot lie." You believe that, don't you? *(Notice, I have switched from the student to them, and I almost always get a positive response to that question.)* It also tells us "God cannot look upon man's sin with approval." Consequently, God cannot overlook our sin. God's holy nature demands righteousness.

I then say, "The important question we must ask is, 'What's the solution to this problem?'" *Usually there is no answer and I continue,* I guess, one solution would be to never sin. But, so far I have never met anyone who has been successful with that plan. So what's the solution? What do you think it is?

I usually pause here a little to find out if they understand the Gospel. Occasionally, someone will respond, "I guess you have to have faith. When they say that, I probe by asking, "What difference would that make?" What I am doing is trying to find out whether they understand that Jesus died as their substitute and paid for their sin.

Finally, I continue on, Let's take a look at God's solution for our problem. While God is holy, He also has infinite love for us. Because of His great love for us, He provided a solution for the spiritual death and separation from God that our sin has produced. The Bible tells us that God sent Jesus Christ to die on the cross so that we can have our fellowship restored with Him. But, this restoration of fellowship with God did not compromise God's holiness. Rather, it satisfied His holiness by giving us a new righteous life that He provides for us through Jesus Christ.

As I say this, I draw an arrow going down from the line under Holy God to the line above Sinful Man, and add a cross bar to turn it into a cross. I continue on.

Religion, philosophy, and ethics have been defined as man's effort to reach God. When God sent Jesus, it was God's love reaching out to us. But, God did not violate the demands of His holy nature by ignoring our sin. Rather, through Jesus, God fulfilled those demands and, by His death on the cross, expressed His great love for us. Romans 5:8 tells us, **"But God proves His love for us, in that while we were yet sinners, Christ died for us."**

The Old Testament in the Bible helps us understand how God accomplished this. When a Jew sinned, the Scriptures instructed him to bring a lamb that was perfect without any blemish, to the tabernacle or the temple. He was commanded to lay his hands on the head of the lamb, to pray, and then to kill the lamb. The priest then took the blood of the lamb and sprinkled it on the altar.

When a faithful Jew laid his hands on the head of the lamb, I believe it was to dramatize two things. First, it was a picture of identification. He was saying, "God, I want You to see me and this lamb as one!" Second, it was a picture of transference. He was saying, "God, all that is true of me is true of this lamb, and all that is true of this lamb is true of me." Making it personal, if all that is true of you is true of the lamb, what would happen to your sin if you laid your hands on the lamb?

I wait for a response and usually they say, "My sin would be transferred to the lamb." *If they don't respond, I supply the answer, and then continue on.*

That's right. It would be transferred to the lamb! Then the lamb must be killed. God, being absolutely holy, had to deal with sin in an absolute way. Hebrews 9:22 tells us, **"...without the shedding of blood there is no forgiveness for sin."**

This is part of what many theologians call, "the scarlet cord of redemption." This cord weaves its way through the Bible. Isaiah chapter 53, a Scripture speaking prophetically of the promised Messiah, tells us: **"All we like sheep have gone astray, we have turned each one to his own ways, but the Lord has laid**

on Him the sin of us all. And that, **... He poured out his soul as an offering for sin."**

I then put out both of my hands in front of me, with the ballpoint pen I am using in my right hand, and say, "Let's say, 'This pen is my sin.'" *As I am saying this, I gently wave my right hand with the pen in it up and down and repeat,* Isaiah said, **"All we like sheep have gone astray, we have turned each one to his own ways, but the Lord has laid on Him the sin of us all ... He poured out his soul an offering for sin."** *As I say this, I move my right hand over in an arc, place the pen in my left hand, and close my left hand around the pen as I say,* ***"He poured out his soul an offering for sin."*** *I then continue.*

Centuries later, Jesus came to John the Baptist, and John said some words you have probably heard in Handel's Messiah. He pointed to Jesus and said, **"Behold the Lamb of God who takes away the sin of the world!"**

Jesus also taught this when he said, **"The Son of Man** (*I insert as an explanation,* 'one of His favorite names for Himself') **came not to be ministered unto, but to minister and give His life a ransom for the many."** The word "ransom" tells of "a payment to release a captive," and the word "for" in the original language meant "in the place of."

Later, while He was on the cross, the last words Jesus said were, **"It is finished!"** These were the exact words that were used in that day to write across the face of a bill, **"PAID IN FULL."**

In big bold letters, I write beneath "Wages = Death" on my paper ***PAID IN FULL!*** *This is the truth I want to drive home as strongly as possible.*

Two truths that I make sure they understand:

1. God cannot overlook their sin

2. Jesus Paid in full the penalty for their sin

In other words, when Jesus died on the cross, He took our place and paid in full the price for our sin, releasing us from bondage to our sin, and making it possible for us to come into fellowship with God. But, our fellowship with God is not based on our personal goodness. Rather, it rests on the righteousness God provides for us, as a free gift, through Jesus Christ.

I follow with my favorite illustration of the atonement. Its purpose is to bring all of the parts of my witness together:

Let me illustrate this in a way that has really helped me understand this important truth. The national hero of Chechnya, a province of the former Soviet Union, was a man named Chemiel. During the Russian revolution, he led a band of men, women and children who resisted the Czar and carried out guerrilla attacks on the Czar's army. Chemiel's group had strict rules of conduct, including a rule that said, "Thou shall not steal!" The penalty for violating this rule was 40 lashes with a whip.

One day, stealing broke out in their camp. A few days later, they found out who did the stealing. The thief was Chemiel's mother! Consequently, Chemiel had a major problem. If he was to have justice, he had to give the command and watch as his mother, whom he loved, was lashed 40 times with a whip.

Chemiel knew he would not be able to discipline anyone else if he did not have his mother whipped, that they would lose their ability to operate effectively as a unit, and that the Czar's army might capture them all. Finally, he came to the conclusion that justice had to be served, he had them bring out his mother, he gave the command, and they began to lash her.

But, after the third lash, Chemiel found his answer. He had them stop. He took his mother's place and took the remaining thirty-seven lashes on his own back. This is an example of a man's love for his mother, but the Bible tells us that "... God so loved the world that He gave His only begotten Son, that whoever believes in Him will not perish, but will have everlasting life."

I always end this illustration with the following to eliminate the perception of many unbelievers that Christians are self-righteous. This is very, very important!

Properly comprehended, there is no boasting in Christianity. In Ephesians 2:8-9, the Bible says, **"For it is by grace** (which means unmerited favor) **you have been saved, through faith, and this not from yourself, it is the gift of God, not by works so that no one can boast."**

I see myself as being just like Chemiel's mother. Because of what she did, her son had to take the lashes on his back, and because of what I have done; Jesus had to die on the cross. But, Chemiel's mother could hold her head high because her son had taken the lashes for her. So also, I can hold my head high because Jesus, who loves me, has paid in full the penalty for my sin. I know I am forgiven through Christ's death on the cross, and when I die, I know I will enter God's presence because the righteousness of Jesus Christ was given to me as a free gift.

The Apostle Paul explained this in II Corinthians 5:21, when he wrote, **"God made Him** (referring to Christ) **who had no sin, to be sin for us, so that we might become the righteousness of God in Him."** That's great news! My sin was transferred to Jesus, who died as my substitute and satisfied the demands of God's holiness. Then, because of His love, His righteousness was given to me as a free gift.

When Jesus spoke to a religious man named Nicodemus, He explained that everyone must have two births to have eternal life. We all had a natural birth, but we also need a new, spiritual birth. Jesus said, **"Except a man be born again, he cannot enter the kingdom of God ... Ye must be born again!"** This new birth comes through placing our faith in Jesus. The Apostle John wrote in I John 5:11-13: **"And this is the testimony: God has given us eternal life and this life is in His Son. He who has the Son, has life; he who does not have the Son of God, does not have life. I write these things ... that you may know that you have eternal life."**

The word Gospel means "good news." It is G*ood News* that through trusting in Jesus Christ as Savior, you can be "born again" and have assurance of eternal life, a life eternally in fellowship with God. Best of all, it is absolutely free. All you have to do is place your faith in the resurrected Jesus as having died on the cross in your place and for your sin.

Prayer is just talking to God. Through a simple prayer of faith, you can receive Jesus as your Savior and partake of His promise of eternal life. The important thing is not the words you pray, rather the attitude of your heart. But, there are some things that you should include in your prayer.

I then list about four things that they should include in their salvation prayer and read them as I am writing.

1. Confess MY sin and guilt to God.

2. Thank God for sending Jesus to die on the cross for MY sin.

3. Ask Jesus to come and live in ME as MY Savior and Lord.

I insert: Notice that I am putting this in the first person for you. Finally, God would not lie to you so you should ...

4. Thank God for hearing and answering MY prayer.

When I have finished, my sheet of paper looks something like the page to the right: ⟶

After writing out the points in the suggested prayer, I ask, "Is there any reason you would not want to make this prayer, your prayer, right now and receive Jesus as your Savior? You would like too, wouldn't you?" If they say yes, I lead them in the prayer.

I sometimes add: When one accepts Jesus as Savior, it is the beginning of a journey with God during this life that continues on into eternity. It is often compared to a marriage. When a man and woman commit themselves to one another in marriage, it begins a long relationship that should be a growing relationship. Just as a couple must spend time with one another in marriage; so also, we grow in our love for God as we have fellowship with Him. If you spend time with God in prayer and Bible study, and have fellowship with other believers, you will find your relationship with God and Christian friends will greatly enrich your life.

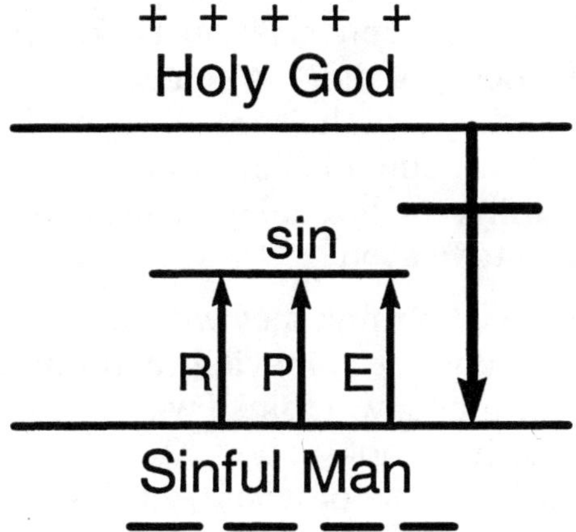

Romans 3:23

All have Sinned

Romans 6:23

Wages = Death

PAID IN FULL

1. Confess MY sin and guilt to God.
2. Thank God for sending Jesus to die on the cross for MY sin.
3. Ask Jesus to come and live in ME as MY Savior and Lord.
4. Thank God for hearing and answering MY prayer.

If they are not yet ready to accept Christ, I often go back to the original question I used to get into the conversation by commenting: When we began this conversation, I asked you, "What would happen to you when you die?" When I ask this question, some people think that they pull the cord, the show is over and that is the end of it. Most people believe in a life after death. Some admit that they think they would go to hell, and others think, or hope, they will go to heaven.

Of the people who think they will go to heaven, I find that the focus of their answer is inevitably in one of two different directions. Either they say, "I think I will go to heaven as a result of what I have, or have not, done." Or they say, "I know that I will go to heaven because of what God did for me when Jesus died on the cross." The focus of their answer either looks to themselves, or it looks to what God has done for them.

It has been interesting to see the response to these comments from those who originally focused on themselves. About 80% will interrupt and say, "I gave the wrong answer, didn't I?" *I respond by saying,* "Yes you did. And if your hope is to make it to heaven as a result of what you do or do not do, you will not make it." *When I get this response, I know I have probably helped to "make a disciple (a learner) as I was going." If you have already asked them to pray to receive Jesus, and they said they are not ready, after such a confession, don't be afraid to ask,* "Are you sure that you would not like to place your faith in Jesus right now?"

It is important that you are sensitive to their response at the end of your presentation. The natural closing to your sharing with them is to challenge them to ask Jesus to come and live in them as his or her Savior and Lord.

It is an awesome thing to see someone pray to receive Jesus as their Savior. Consequently, it is not always easy to ask them to trust in Jesus. But, becoming a Christian is a decision of the will. For some, the most important part of your presentation to them will be when you ask, "Is there any reason that you would not like to ask Jesus to come and live in you, right now?

I must admit that I do not always ask people to pray to receive Jesus at the end of my witness. Sometimes I challenge them to get down on their knees before they go to bed that night, and make this prayer (pointing at the list on the paper). A very large majority of the people with whom I have shared the Gospel, ask for the piece of paper that I have used in the explanation.

Sometimes you will witness to someone, and they will honestly tell you that this (the Gospel of grace) is a new concept for them, and they need to think about it for a few days. Recently, I had the opportunity to share the Gospel with a man as his Christian wife listened in. He gave me a "this is something new that I have to think about" answer, when I asked him if he wanted to accept Jesus as his Savior. We were about to enter the hot and humid months here in Houston, and the Lord gave me a new response.

Without thinking, I said to him, "Gary, you need to give very serious consideration to how you are going to respond to God's offer of forgiveness through Jesus. If you just ignore the question, you will ultimately find that you have rejected His offer. And remember, this is a really important decision, because the decision you make, one way or the other, will determine whether you spend eternity with God in heaven, or whether you spend it in a place that is desperately in need of air conditioning.

Both he and his wife had to laugh. I am sure he understood my warning! As a resident of Houston, he probably will not forget it. I trust that if he procrastinates about the Gospel and complains about the heat, his wife will remind him by saying, "If you think this is hot, just wait till you get to that place that desperately needs air-conditioning."

When someone does pray to receive Jesus, the presentation is not over. It is time to make sure they have assurance of their salvation. If I have a Bible with me I open it to Hebrews 13:5 and say:

Let's take a look at a passage in the Bible. In Hebrews 13:5 it says, "...for He has said, "I will never leave you, nor forsake you." *Then I ask,* "Did you just ask Jesus to come and live in you as your Savior?" *When I get the yes answer, I continue,* "Would He lie to you?" *When I get the no answer, I ask,* "Then where is He right now?" *I want them to tell me that He is in their life, and continue on.* Now, notice what Jesus said in Hebrews 13:5. Let's say you wake up tomorrow and don't feel good. Is Jesus still in your life? *If they hesitate, I again ask,* "Would He lie to you?"

The series of questions and answers in the previous paragraph depend, of course, on the response. Sometime a question must be asked more than one to get the right response. But sometimes, when they finally give the right answer, it is like a light of faith just flashed on.

After getting the correct answers from Hebrews 13:5, I turn to I John 5: and read verses 11-13: "And this is the record, that God has given to us eternal life, and this life is in His Son. He that hath the Son hath life, and he that hath not the Son of God hath not life. These things have I written unto you that ye may know that you have eternal life..." *and ask them,* "Do you have the Son?" *When they answer yes, then I ask,* "Then what do you have?" *The goal is to get them to confess that they have received Jesus Christ and have eternal life. Again, sometimes during this assurance phase it is almost like a light comes on, and I have often wondered whether the salvation faith came during the prayer, or when "the light came on." Consequently, this is a very important part of a witness.*

As mentioned above, my presentation is merely one way to present the Gospel. Feel free to use part, or all of it, in your personal presentation. The important thing is that you take the time to prepare a way to share Christ that you are comfortable with, and that fits your personality. It might be a good idea to check out several presentations from people who are effective in sharing their faith to find one that fits you. Many effective witnesses for Jesus have borrowed parts of their presentations from several sources. If you say things differently, that's O.K. Just, put the thoughts in your own words, have a plan, and use it.

Occasionally, when teaching personal evangelism, someone will say, "I don't like the idea of having a canned presentation." My response is, "Don't think of it as a canned presentation. Think of it as a planned presentation."

"If your preacher walked into the pulpit without a plan for his sermon, he would ramble, and not feed his congregation the spiritual food it needs. Your preacher prepares a planned presentation every week, and then presents it to many people. You may not have the opportunity to speak to a big crowd. But, you do have opportunities to speak to many people, one by one. You need a good planned presentation for those opportunities so that you can give them the spiritual food they desperately need."

Let me suggest that after you prepare your Gospel presentation *(again, you can borrow anything from this book that you like)*, practice it several times with a close Christian friend. After you use it several times, your presentation of it will become very natural."

After preparing your Gospel message and sharing it person to person several times, it will flow easily and become natural.

So, get ready to share your faith. Because, if you are prepared to show and tell, God will give you some divine appointments so that the Gospel will be clearly explained to people whom He wants to trust in Jesus. And "as you are going ..." you will "make disciples."

Chapter Seven

Ripe Fruit

My sheep hear my voice, and I know them, and they follow me. And I give unto them eternal life; and they shall never perish, neither shall any man pluck them out of my hand.

Jesus, John 10:27-28

When you make an appointment with skeptical male college students to talk to them about Jesus, it is not uncommon to be stood up. As waited for a student, with whom I had an appointment, I chatted with a coed, named Nancy, who was seated behind a table where she was recruiting students for the Washington Educational Association. Before long, I guessed that my appointment would probably not show up.

As I waited, I asked Nancy if she would read something and tell me what she thought of it. She said "Sure," and I handed her a copy of the Four Spiritual Laws. It took her a few minutes to read through the booklet, and when she looked up I asked, "What did you think of it? Does it make sense to you?" She responded, "Yes it does." I asked, "Have you ever received Jesus Christ as your Savior?" She said, "No, I haven't." I asked, "Would you like to?" She said, "Yes I would." I suggested that she make the prayer in the book, her prayer, and Nancy bowed her head and prayed to receive Christ.

While we chatted, as I continued to wait for my appointment, I gave her a copy of The Collegiate Challenge a magazine published in those days by Campus Crusade, and invited her to come to a meeting we were having the following evening. Later that day, I gave Nancy's name to a Christian student in her dorm, and suggested she stop by and encourage this new believer. The following evening, Nancy came to the meeting with the coed from her dorm.

After the meeting, Nancy came up to me and said, "You know that magazine you gave me? Someone else gave me a copy of that same magazine last summer." I asked who gave it to her and she responded, "I live in Tacoma, and last summer I dated a guy in the Army who was stationed at Fort Lewis, and he gave it to me." I asked if she knew where he was now, and she responded, "Yes, he is in Vietnam." I suggested that she write him a letter to tell him what happened.

A couple of weeks later, Nancy came to me and excitedly told me that she had received a reply from her letter to the soldier in Vietnam. In the letter, he told her that in Vietnam, on the other side of the world, he had been praying for her to come to know Jesus as her Savior.

I have often heard that there is a lot of praying that goes on in a foxhole, but his was a very special prayer. They continued to write. Nancy decided to go with us to a spring break conference at Arrowhead Springs in California, and on the way down to the conference, she talked a whole carload of us into driving an hour out of our way so she could stop by Yuba City and meet her soldier's parents.

The Lord protected this young soldier in Vietnam; he later returned, one thing lead to another, and Nancy married him. The last I heard of them, they were at Moody Bible Institute, preparing to go to the mission field.

The believer who prays is a vital part of the ministry to many who accept Christ.

It is not uncommon for those who share Christ with someone to "take the credit" when the person comes to know Jesus. But, we should also give credit to the person who prayed for them -- they are often a vital part in a decision to believe in Jesus as their Savior. All I did was ask Nancy a few questions and suggested that she pray to receive Christ. Her future husband had spent nights in a foxhole praying for her to come to know Jesus. God answered his prayer; I was merely incidental to the process.

Nancy was ripe fruit. It is obvious that the Lord had been preparing her for that day in the Student Union. I don't know if she recruited many students for the Washington Educational Association, but she joined something far more important. She became a member of God's army that is spreading the Gospel all over the world.

In I Corinthians, chapter three, we learn from the Apostle Paul that some plant, others water, but it is God who brings the increase. Always remember that it is usually a process, involving several witnesses or prayer warriors, for someone to come to know Christ as their Savior.

I'm sure that Nancy had heard about Jesus, even before dating her future husband. That summer in Tacoma, he shared with her and gave her a Christian magazine to read. Most important of all, he continued to pray for her. When I met her, the way had been prepared and she was ripe fruit, ready to receive Jesus. I just had the privilege of picking that ripe fruit. The appointment I had made stood me up, but the divine appointment God made for me was right on time.

Thank God when He leads you to ripe fruit.
Plant, water, or fertilize the green fruit.
But, don't bruise it.

Sometimes our role is that of a planter. At other times, we water or fertilize. Occasionally, if we talk to enough people, God will reward us with the privilege of harvesting. If the fruit is green, we should not bruise it. But, it does not always appear to be ripe when it is. It is easy to ask questions to get into a conversation about the Lord. On the other hand, I have learned that it is often very hard to get the words out and ask the most important question of all; "Would you like to ask Jesus to come and live in you as your Savior, RIGHT NOW?"

There are many ways that question can be asked. Some of our Campus Crusade staff women would describe a prayer to female college students that went something like: "I Sally, take you Jesus, to be my personal Savior. To have and to hold, from this day forward, and on throughout all eternity." Then they would ask if they "would like to make this prayer, your prayer, right now."

Bob Reese was the manager of the local cable TV company, and his wife, Margaret, was a real estate agent who worked in an office with my wife, Jane. At the time, Margaret was a workaholic, and one of the top agents in the Bryan-College Station market. But, their marriage was falling apart.

There were several Christians in the real estate office, and one day Bob stopped by and bemoaned to one of them some problems he and Margaret were having in their marriage. It was suggested to him, "Jane Prall's husband is a minister; why don't you drop by his office and talk to him?"

Later that day, Bob stopped by my office, I shared the Gospel with him, and he accepted Christ. We started meeting a couple of times a week, and he started attending our church. I also suggested to Bob that he would enjoy a weekly men's Bible study taught by Aaron Schapery, a retired gentleman who was a Messianic Jew and a member of our church. In the next few months, Bob began to grow in his faith like a weed.

Knowing Margaret a bit, and hearing about her from my wife, I suggested to Bob that he could not go home and preach to her. The verse in First Peter, directed to wives, that their husbands must be "won without a word," was good advice for him.

I will never forget the first time Margaret attended our church with Bob. At the time, Grace Bible Church, where I was pastor, was still in a dumpy little building in an old section of Bryan (the next year we relocated to a new building a few blocks from Texas A&M in College Station.) Margaret was a tall stately redhead. As I looked out over the congregation, she stood out like a sore thumb, and frankly, she looked a little bit out of place to me (though I was of course excited that she there).

A couple of months later, there was a marriage conference in Houston with Howard Hendricks and Tim LaHaye as speakers. My wife talked it up with some of the other female agents in her office, and several of them convinced their husbands to attend it. Bob had already decided to attend the conference, and the other agents urged Margaret to go with him. Initially she refused, but she finally gave in.

About a week after the conference, I was driving home on a street in a residential area, and Bob was coming from the other direction. He signaled me to stop, rolled down the window of his car, and excitedly told me that Margaret had accepted the Lord. I asked how it happened, and he replied, "Last night, Aaron and Nell Schapery came over to our house for dinner, and Aaron led Margaret to the Lord."

A few weeks later, Margaret told the other Christian agents in her office about her conversation with Aaron. When she explained how he asked her to accept Christ, Margaret described it by saying, "Then he got to the end and put a super close on me!"

Aaron was an enthusiastic and faithful personal evangelist. Knowing him as I did, I have no doubt that he "put a super close on her." Years later, Margaret explained to me what he said when he put that "super close" on her.

Aaron knew that as a real estate agent, Margaret asked people to sign contracts. So, he asked her for her Bible, turned to a blank page in the back, wrote out a salvation prayer as if it was a contract, then asked her to pray and to sign on the dotted line. As she sat there analyzing his sales techniques, she negotiated the most important contract of her life.

As with Nancy, there were several steps in the process whereby Margaret became a Christian. She observed the lives of the Christian agents in her office, she saw her husband's life change, she sat through several of my sermons, and she heard Howard Hendricks and Tim LaHaye speak about a Christian marriage. When she had that divine dinner with Aaron and Nell Schapery, she was ripe fruit, ready to "sign on the dotted line."

Believe me, Margaret's life was transformed. She later left the real estate business, they adopted a son, and she went from being a hardnosed, aggressive real estate agent to a sweet and gentle wife and mother. Richard, the owner of the real estate firm, who had grown up as a preacher's kid, later told me, "I have never seen a miracle before. But I have seen one in Margaret's life."

Our God is a God of miracles. The most amazing miracles of all are the transformed lives of those who come to know Jesus as their Savior, and that He allows you and me to be used as instruments in the miracles He performs in the lives of others. What a privilege. What a joy!

If you are faithful in little things, God may reward you by introducing you to someone whom He has prepared through the efforts of others.

But remember, you need to do your share of the planting and watering. If you are faithful in little things, God may reward you by introducing you to someone whom He has prepared through the efforts of others. After all, He said, "The fields are white unto harvest."

So get ready, be available, and "As you are going..." God may lead you to some ripe fruit at one of your divine appointments. Ask the important questions, "Is there any reason that you would not want to receive Jesus Christ as your Savior -- right now? -- You would like to, wouldn't you?" If you ask those questions often enough, you will undoubtedly experience the joy of seeing God do a miracle as He uses you as His instrument to "Make Disciples."

Chapter Eight
The Harder They Fall

But they heard only, That he which persecuted us in times past now preaches the faith which he once destroyed.
Galatians 1:28

Every Sunday evening, we had a gathering of Christian students at Duke University, that we called College Life. It was well attended, and we always had a warm time of fellowship and sharing. One evening, during the sharing time, a coed told about a specific answer to her prayers.

That same evening, an unbelieving student named Dick Piech wandered into our meeting. After the meeting, he headed back to his dorm and proceeded to badmouth us all over the place. He was a physics major, who was very cynical about religion. As far as he was concerned, we were merely material for his jokes.

That evening, Dick joined a late night bull session, and sarcastically told everyone there about the meeting he had gone to and the "group of stupid Christians" he had met. In particular, he ridiculed the coed's testimony about the answered prayer.

That's not the kind of advertising you usually want, but it worked that time. There was another student in the bull session who said nothing to anyone else, but said to himself, "Boy, that's just what I have been looking for."

Many believers tend to panic when there is a negative reaction toward their witness for Jesus. But the Lord can even use a cynic like Dick to recruit people for his army. The next week, Dick's dorm mate went to our meeting, became an active member of our group, grew in his faith, later went to seminary, and became a Methodist pastor in North Carolina.

My experience has taught me that the harshest critics are often close to coming to know Christ. Frankly, I would rather get an intensely negative response to the Gospel than an apathetic, "so what" response. Like the Apostle Paul before them, those who persecute believers often become the Lord's most powerful advocates, and Dick is a prime example.

When you get a negative response to a witness for Jesus, remember that the Holy Spirit can turn negatives into positives.

Dick continued to attend our meetings for amusement. But, the Holy Spirit convicted him of his need for Jesus, and the next summer he committed his life to Christ. Dick became one of our most enthusiastic witnesses on the Duke campus.

After graduation, Dick went into the U.S. Navy as an officer. Like most naval officers, he began his career in San Diego, California. At the time, Bob Luther, the pastor who had led me to the Lord when he pastored a small church in Aumsville, Oregon, was the pastor of College Avenue Baptist Church in San Diego.

While I had not actually lead Dick to Christ, he had come to know Jesus as a result of our Campus Crusade ministry at Duke, and I had spent a lot of time with him when he was a new Christian. Because I was the director of the ministry that had brought him to Jesus, Dick considered me his "spiritual father." So, when he went to San Diego, he introduced himself to Bob Luther as "your spiritual grandson," and attended College Avenue Baptist Church.

As a young Ensign in the Navy, Dick lived in the Bachelors Officers Quarters. He befriended another young officer, shared the Gospel with him, and he became a Christian. Dick took him to College Avenue Baptist Church, where Bob Luther baptized his spiritual great grandson.

As I was working on this book, I called Bob, who is now semi-retired and lives in Salem, Oregon. He shared with me that while Dick was in San Diego, he also discipled a Lieutenant J.G. who later joined the military staff of Campus Crusade for Christ, and that officer lead a First Class Petty Officer to the Lord who also joined Bob's Church in San Diego.

And ... who knows where this story will end. The generation that was born-again in Oregon, gave birth again in North Carolina; and regenerated itself again and again in California. The First Class Petty officer is now a missionary in Spain. I told Bob Luther, "If you think you were blessed in baptizing your spiritual great grandson in California, just wait till we get to heaven and meet all of the Spaniards."

A few years after Dick left San Diego, I received a letter from him as he was serving on a U.S. Navy vessel in the middle of the Mediterranean Sea. In his letter, Dick wrote that a group of midshipmen from the Naval Academy were assigned to his ship. None of the other officers wanted the responsibility of overseeing them, so Dick volunteered for the job in order to minister to them. Dick led a Bible study for them every evening, and it sounded in his letter like he was holding revival meetings. What a great opportunity. As he was cruising, Dick was making disciples, and there were not a lot of diversions for them out there in the middle of the Mediterranean Sea. One of the midshipmen in that Bible study later became the director of the Officers Christian Fellowship.

Dick later went to medical school and served for many years as a Navy physician. At this writing, he is Director of Health Services for Rutgers University and is an Associate Clinical Professor at Robert Wood Johnson Medical School. Knowing Dick, I am sure there are others who are hearing about Jesus through his witness.

Those who are most cynical, often become dynamic witnesses for Jesus.

Next time you run into an unbelieving cynic like the pre-Christian Dick, don't get discouraged. He may be a dynamic witness for Jesus, just waiting to happen. My observation is that the more cynical they are, the harder they can fall.

Dick was a real blessing to my life, as I am sure he was to Bob Luther. In II Timothy 2:2, the Apostle Paul exhorted us, **"And the things which you have heard from me in the presence of many witnesses, these entrust to faithful men, who will be able to teach others also."**

When you invest time in ministering to new believers, it is exciting to later hear about their ministering to others. So, keep telling people about Jesus. You never know what multiplied impact may be in the making for the Lord. When you get to Glory, I am confident that He will tell you about everything that ultimately happened as a result of your *making disciples, as you were going* in this life.

And don't be surprised if some of those who are most antagonistic to the Gospel accept Christ, and become effective witnesses for Jesus. From the Apostle Paul to many others like Dick, those who have been antagonistic to the Gospel often become dynamic witnesses for Jesus. To adapt a common saying, "The more antagonistic they are, the harder they fall." So *"as you are going,"* don't avoid those who are antagonistic to the Christian faith. Just tell them about the love of Jesus. The Holy Spirit might melt their hearts, and use your witness to help *"make disciples."*

Chapter Nine

Jesus Can Change a Life

Therefore, if any man be in Christ, he is a new creature; old things have passed away; behold, all things have become new.

II Corinthians 5:21

It was time for a vacation, and I returned to my hometown of Salem, Oregon to see my family and friends. Having been a golf bum during high school and college, I dropped by the local country club to say hello to some old friends.

While there, I saw someone I had known since my high school years, though at that time he was a businessman and I was the young kid who worked in the pro shop cleaning clubs. Frank was financially very successful, but was a big drinker who loved to gamble, and was notorious as a womanizer.

When Frank saw me, he said, "Hi Bob, it's good to see you. Stop by my office; I would like to talk to you." I could not help but ask myself, "I wonder why Frank wants to talk to me? He knows what I stand for now."

The next day, I stopped by to see Frank, and he asked me to come into his office. As we chatted, he told me about a young woman whom he had been dating, and how she had broken up with him because she was a Christian. (I thought to myself, "That was a good reason, but she should have considered the fact that Frank was a married man, and had two teenage daughters, before she started dating him.")

Frank continued on and told me that, about a month after she broke up with him, he had a conversation with a man in the locker room at the local YMCA as they were both getting ready for a workout. As they talked about physical fitness, Frank commented, "I try to stay in good shape, but I probably smoke and drink too much." His new acquaintance responded, "I used to smoke and drink too, but I quit." Frank asked him why he quit, and he explained to Frank that he had become a Christian.

After hearing these stories, I assumed that Frank asked me to come to his office for a divine appointment. I pulled a Four Spiritual Laws booklet out of my shirt pocket and said, "Frank, let me go through something and explain some things from the Bible to you." Frank looked at the booklet and responded, "Oh, I have one of those." He opened his desk drawer, pulled out a bunch of Gospel tracts, shuffled through the stack and found his copy of the Four Spiritual Laws.

I said, "That's good, Frank, but let me go through it anyway." He consented, and I took about ten minutes to explain the Gospel to him. At the end of the presentation, I asked Frank if he had ever accepted Christ as his Savior. He responded "No," and I asked him if he would like to pray, right now, and ask Jesus to come and live in him as his Savior.

Frank looked at his watch and said, "Look, I'm already late for an appointment I have in Portland, and I don't want to do this when I'm in a hurry. How long will you be in town?" I explained that I was leaving the following Monday morning and probably would not be back for at least a year. He told me that he was leaving for a convention in Chicago on Saturday, and suggested that we meet on Friday morning. We set the appointment for nine o'clock.

My parent's phone rang at about 8:15 that Friday morning. It was Frank's secretary explaining that Frank did not feel well that day, he was not coming into his office, and thus he had to cancel our appointment.

Later that morning, I went to the office of an attorney who had asked me to stop by and see him. Otto was about Frank's age, and was a strong Christian. When we went into his private office, he said to me, "Frank stopped by to see me and asked me some questions about spiritual things. I know that someone needs to put the bee on him to get him to accept the Lord. When I heard that you were in town, I thought that maybe you were the one to do it."

I told Otto about my conversation with Frank, and how he had canceled our appointment for that morning. Otto said, "I sure wish you could talk to him." I replied, "Otto, I have an idea. I think I will go see Frank at his home." I left Otto's office and immediately drove to Frank's house.

Frank lived in a big house on a hill overlooking the city. You had to enter from the rear, and there was a tall hedge and a high gate next to the sidewalk. When I opened the gate, there was Frank, in his bathing suit, catching some rays by his swimming pool. He looked a little embarrassed, faked a couple of coughs, and explained that he had a cold so he did not go to his office. I have to admit, I had to work hard to keep from laughing as "sick Frank" stood there in his swimming trunks.

We engaged in a little small talk, and then I said to him, "Frank, let me tell you what you are thinking." He looked at me as if he was thinking, "O.K. wise guy, how would you know what I am thinking." But instead, he said, "What do you mean by what I am thinking?" I replied, "Frank, you are thinking, 'Here I am, getting ready to go to a convention in Chicago. This is not the right time to accept the Lord.'"

With a surprised look on his face, Frank said, "That's exactly what I am thinking." Then, as he pointed at himself with his thumb, he almost shouted, "I KNOW ME! And, I know what is going to happen when I get to Chicago. This is definitely not the time to accept Christ."

Frank almost shouted, "I know me!" Deep down inside, everyone "knows me." All have tried to change sinful parts of their lives, by their own power, and all have failed.

I said to him, "Frank, let me explain something to you. Accepting Christ is not something where you must clean up your life before you come to Him. Frank, you can't change your life. You have already tried that, and it has not worked. What you need to do is go to God in prayer and say, "God, I have blown it. I know that I am not capable of making any changes in my life, so it is all up to You. I know I am a sinner and need Jesus as my Savior. But it is up to You to make any changes, because I can't do it. So, Jesus, with that as an understanding, I ask you to forgive me and come and live in me as my Savior."

With tears in his eyes, Frank said, "If that's the way it is, I am ready right now." He bowed his head and asked Jesus to come and live in him as his Savior. I'm sure the angels in heaven were rejoicing. I sure was!

About a year later, I was back in Salem and had lunch with a friend. John was a stockbroker in Salem, and a strong Christian. He shared with me that earlier in the day he had taken a coffee break with a group of men. During their time together, he happened to mention that he had gone to a Bible study early that morning.

One of the men asked, "Who all was at the study?" John listed the names of the men, and when he mentioned Frank's name, he was interrupted by one of the men who asked in amazement, "What was Frank doing at a Bible study? I can't believe that he would be at a Bible study." One of the other men, who was Jewish, responded before John could answer, "Oh, I can believe that Frank was at a Bible study. He has changed, and so has his wife. I can believe it!"

About a year ago, over twenty years after Frank accepted Christ; I was on the phone with an old friend from high school who is now a businessman in Salem. I asked him how Frank was doing spiritually. He responded, "Well, the last thing I heard was that Frank was telling people around town, 'I can't believe that I spent New Year's Eve in church.'"

We often look at someone we know well and assume, "That person would never be interested in spiritual things, or there is no way that he or she would ever accept Christ." This is particularly true when the person appears to be successful in other areas of their life. I must admit that I thought that way about Frank. If he had not taken the initiative to ask me to stop by his office, I would have been reluctant to try to share the Gospel with him. We should always remember that God delights in making trophies of grace out of the most rebellious sinners.

God delights in making trophies of His grace from rebellious sinners.

Again, I am reminded that when people come to Christ, the Lord often uses the witness of many people. The Lord used the testimony of several people in Frank's life -- the Christian woman who broke up with him, the man in the locker room, his friend Otto, whom Frank knew was a committed Christian, and probably others.

> **Neither the one who plants, nor the one who waters is anything, but God who causes the growth. Now he who plants and he who waters are one, but each will receive his reward according to his own labor.** (I Corinthians 3:7-8)

We also need to remember that there are people who think they need to clean up their lives before coming to Jesus. While we may sing to them "Just as I am," sometimes we need to explain to them that they can't clean up their own lives. But, while they can't change their lives, Jesus is in the life changing business.

So, *as you are going*, be sure that you let those potential *disciples* know the Good News that Jesus not only died for their sins, but that He can make them new.

Chapter Ten

Never use this word!

LET NO MAN DECEIVE HIMSELF. IF ANY MAN AMONG YOU SEEMETH TO BE WISE IN THIS WORLD, LET HIM BECOME A FOOL, THAT HE MAY BE WISE.

I CORINTHIANS 3:18

Harry was Jewish. I spent several hours over a couple of days sharing the Gospel and Christian evidences with him. He promised to go home and think about all that I had shared with him, and to come back the next day and give me his response to the information I had shared with him.

I met him the next day in front of the Student Union. He had a couple of friends with him, and he said, "What you have told me makes sense. You have given me a lot of strong evidence. But, I have decided that I need absolute proof before I accept Christ, and you have not given it to me."

I smiled at Harry and asked, "Harry, can I ask you a few questions?" He said, "Sure." I continued on, "Harry, you like to be consistent in life, don't you?" He said, "Yes." I then asked, "Harry, have you ever flown in an airplane?" He again said, "Yes." Then I asked, "How much do you know about aerodynamics?" He replied, "I don't know anything about aerodynamics." To that, I playfully responded, "Harry, I can't believe that you would ride in an airplane when you don't have proof for all of the laws of aerodynamics. After all, Harry, you are a guy who needs absolute proof before you will act."

His friends laughed at him as he shuffled his feet, and I continued on, "Harry, have you ever taken an aspirin?" He again answered, "Yes." So I asked, "How much do you know about how an aspirin works?" He admitted that he did not know anything about how an aspirin works. So, I continued on, "Well, don't feel too bad Harry, because medical science does not fully understand how or why an aspirin works. But, if you want to be consistent in life, you should never take an aspirin. Because Harry, you are a guy who needs absolute proof. As a matter of fact, Harry, all you better do is sit around and vegetate, because you can't have absolute proof for anything."

Harry did not accept Christ that day, and I don't know whether he has since then. Hopefully, every time he rides in an airplane or takes an aspirin for the rest of his life, he will remember the illustration. I do know that he will not have an excuse at the judgment day, as he understood the Gospel message and realized that the evidence for the claims of Christ is strong. He is another whom I will check on when I get to Heaven.

If you are a consistent witness for Jesus, you will probably plant a more seeds, and do more watering, than you will harvest.

You might be saying to yourself, "Bob has a lot of people to check on when he gets to heaven." If "as you are going" through life, you are a consistent witness for Jesus, it is likely that you will plant a lot more seeds, and do a lot more watering, than you will ever harvest. That has been my experience. As I have mentioned in other chapters, coming to know Jesus as Savior usually follows several influences. We each need to do what we can, when we can, and leave the results up to the Lord. As that great philosopher Yoggi Berra expressed it, "It ain't over until it's over!" So always remember, God is able, and He is faithful. When you witness and the response is negative, don't be discouraged. Rather, thank the Lord that you had the privilege of planting or watering a seed.

If you witness on a college campus, you quickly learn that there is a word you should never use. It is the word PROVE. If you tell a skeptical student who has taken a logic course that you can *prove* that the Bible is the Word of God, or that Jesus is the Messiah, it's like putting a noose around your neck.

The word *prove*, or *proof*, was used by the ancient Greek philosophers when they developed deductive logic and reasoning. A logical syllogism may be proven to be valid. But, it can never be proven to be true. The truthfulness of a conclusion is always dependent on the truthfulness of its presuppositions. Thus, from a philosophical standpoint, nothing can ever be proven to be true.

A logical syllogism may be proven to be valid. But, it can never be proven to be true.

If you say, "I believe this," someone can always ask, "Why do you believe it?" When you give a reason, again they can ask you, "Why?" If anyone is asked why enough times, about anything they believe, their only recourse is to finally answer, "I just believe that by faith." This is not only true of Christianity, but it is true of everything.

When Rusty Wright was a student at Duke University, he heard me use my aspirin illustration several times. Late one night, Rusty was in a fraternity bull session, and a student named Pete commented, "The problem with you Christians is that you can't prove anything." Rusty replied, "Pete, have you ever taken an aspirin?" and pointed out the inconsistency in his criticism. Pete sat there quietly listening, and a little later another fraternity brother, named Jeff, joined the group. After a few minutes, Jeff said, "The problem with Christians is that you guys can't prove anything." Before Rusty could open his mouth, Pete jumped back in the conversation and said, "Jeff, have you ever taken an aspirin?" and he gleefully made "his point."

We are Christians by faith. But, that term is misunderstood by most of the unbelievers in the world. They interpret *faith* to mean, "There is no good reason to believe this, but I have no other good options, so I will take a blind leap into the dark and believe it anyway." *That is not Christian faith!*

As Christians, our faith rests on strong evidence. I believe the evidence for Christianity is so strong, that when it is examined with an open mind, a thinking person has to conclude that the evidence goes way beyond what is needed to remove all reasonable doubt. (I should add that just because someone is an academic, or even a professor, it does not mean he or she has an open mind.)

**We are Christians by faith.
Our faith rests on strong evidence.**

One evening, after helping teach at a Lay Institute for Evangelism at Allendale Baptist Church in Austin, Texas, three of us headed down to the Night Hawk restaurant, a few blocks from the University of Texas campus, to get a bite to eat. At the booth across the aisle from us, there were two young couples. Both girls had on nametags from a high school debate tournament that was being held on the campus, and we found out that the guys were freshmen at the University of Texas who, the previous year, had been members of the same high school debate team with the girls.

As we chatted across the aisle with them, someone in our group said, "You must like to debate, so let's have a debate." They laughed and he continued on, "I'll tell you what. Let's have a debate as to whether Jesus Christ is the Son of God and thus the only way to get to Heaven. We will take the affirmative position."

One of the male students jumped at the challenge and began the debate. I must admit that it was not a fair debate, because it turned out to be three against one -- the two girls and the other college freshman at their table just listened. I also must say that this University of Texas student was an excellent debater, and that he had some of the better questions and objections that I have heard. And ... boy did he fight hard.

We first explained the Gospel and some Christian evidences and then debated back and forth for over an hour. Finally, this student surprised us by saying, "Well, the Christians back at my dorm are going to laugh when they hear about this. I have now lost another debate on Christianity." Then he made a very interesting observation. He said, "You know, this is not a fair debate.

It's not a fair question for debate, because the evidence is all on your side. If someone knows the case for Christianity, it is just not a fair debate."

Wow! What an observation. He admitted that he had wanted us to say we could prove something, but we did not go for the trap. He also admitted that while he had not yet accepted Christ, he was getting close. When we challenged him to the debate, he had decided to give it one more try to see if he could find flaws in the evidence for Christianity.

Knowing that he was going to admit what had happened at the Night Hawk to the Christians in his dorm, we did not even ask him to pray to receive Christ that night. I, for one, figured that privilege should go to those who had been witnessing to him for several months. He is one who I don't think I need to check on. I am confident that he will be there in heaven.

The sequence I usually follow when I have an opportunity to share the Gospel with a skeptic is to first make a transition, usually by asking the questions I described earlier in this book, and then to present the Gospel. It's rare that I go into Christian evidences prior to explaining the Gospel. Making sure they understand whom Jesus is and what He did for them on the cross is my top priority. I try to not get sidetracked.

Put the evidence on hold until after you have presented Christ crucified.

Then, if they are not ready to trust in Jesus, or have questions or objections, I explain that nothing can be proven, but I am a Christian by faith based on evidence. I say, "If you will examine it, I believe that you will find the evidence for Christianity is very strong." I then challenge them to examine the evidence. If the setting is appropriate, I share with them some of the information in the following chapters.

When questions are asked, I do not hesitate to answer some questions, **"I don't know."** If their response implies, "If you don't know, that proves Christianity is not true," I come back with my airplane or aspirin illustration. Just because we don't know the answer to a question does not prove there is not an answer. This is true in every area of knowledge.

Don't be afraid to humbly say, "I don't know." The beauty of answering, "I don't know," is that you don't have to defend it. But, don't let anyone get away with saying, or implying, "Because you don't have an answer to my question, that proves that Christianity is false." That is like saying, "Because you don't know why an aspirin works, that means it can not help me if I get a headache." Remember, only God has all of the answers.

When you say, "I don't know," you don't have to defend it.

Even if I feel I have a good answer, I often delay answering it until after I present Christian evidences by saying, " That is a good question, and I will be happy to try and answer it for you. But it is important that we first look at some evidences for Christianity, then I can answer you question in that context. Is that O.K.?" Usually they agree, and I proceed to the evidences. As I have mentioned before, it is important that we keep our objective in mind as we tell people about Jesus.

The next few chapters will share with you how I present Christian evidences. Mine is not the only way to do it. Feel free to use any of my materials in any way you choose. But, **"as you are going..."** and **"Making Disciples,"** don't ever say:

"I can PROVE it."

Chapter Eleven

He Has Risen, Indeed!

But if there be no resurrection of the dead, then is Christ not risen: And if Christ is not risen, then is our preaching vain, and your faith is vain.

I Corinthians 15:13-14

We were holding a planning session for a training conference. The director for the conference was Paul Eshleman, who at that time was the Campus Director for Campus Crusade at the University of Wisconsin. Paul asked, "Who has something we can use for another seminar?"

I responded, "I have a message on the resurrection of Jesus Christ that we could use." Paul looked at me and said, "Yes, I have heard that message. One of my staff members up in Wisconsin got a tape of your message and memorized it word for word." Then he added with a smile, "He does a better job of presenting it than you do!"

I laughed and said, "That's O.K. After all, I stole everything in that message from other people." As an old saying among writers goes, "If you steal something from one person, it is plagiarism. But, if you steal it from a lot of people, it's research." I am sure that Paul's staff member spiced up my *research* with a few thoughts he got from other people, so we will call his efforts *research*. And, I encourage you to use the information in this book in your research as you diligently prepare to be a more effective witness for Jesus.

In this chapter, we will look at the evidence for the resurrection of Jesus, and in the following two chapters we will look at the evidence from fulfilled prophecy. If you do not feel qualified to present either of these cases, the same information is in four page letters that are a part of a packet of Witnessing Letters (permission is granted to make copies of these letters). ISBN 0-9657835-3-7-- available through Christian bookstores.

Just as I had Nancy read something (in Chapter Five), and it moved her to accept Christ, so also, you can use these letters by asking someone to read them and give you their opinion.

As mentioned in the previous chapter, nothing can be proven absolutely. But when properly presented, the presuppositions for the evidence for the resurrection of Jesus are hard for a skeptic to challenge. And, it is not necessary to establish that truth to effectively present the evidence.

While I believe that a strong case can be made that the Bible is the Word of God, I rarely present it to unbelievers. When dealing with skeptics, it is important that you choose your "battle fields." The battle over the nature and extent of the inspiration of the Bible can easily degenerate into questions about apparent contradictions, etc. That is not a battle I want to wage. There are good answers, and it is important that we deal with the hard questions for the benefit of believers. But with unbelievers, the old saying is true that, "The best defense is a good offense." As I wrote in an earlier chapter, the Bible is a sword, is a sword, is a sword. You don't have to prove it. Just use it!

The best defense is a good offense is also true of the Bible. Don't try to prove it -- just use it.

There are books that examine the evidence for the resurrection of Jesus in great detail. It would be good for you to examine such a book. But, from a practical standpoint, most people will not let you bend their ears for an hour-long explanation of the evidence for the resurrection.

Consequently, my presentation of the evidence for the resurrection is not exhaustive. Rather, I have selected certain parts of the evidence and organized it in a way that will communicate to a skeptic in a relatively short period of time. Notice that this explanation leaves it to the skeptic to answer the tough questions. Let's take a look at this selective examination of the evidence for the resurrection. The following is an explanation of the resurrection that I have presented verbally, in a conversational way, many times:

The question before us is, "Did Jesus Christ really rise from the grave?" The importance of this question is emphasized by the Apostle Paul in his first letter to the Corinthians, where he wrote "... if Christ has not been raised, our preaching is useless and so is your faith." Put another way, "If Jesus Christ did not rise from the grave, then the Christian faith is a waste of time, a bad joke." But, if Jesus Christ did actually rise from the grave, it validates His personal claims, and there are eternal implications for each of us, implications so vital that it would be foolish for you to ignore this question.

If Jesus Christ arose from the grave, there are eternal implications that no one should ignore.

A second question logically follows, "Is there evidence that can establish, beyond a reasonable doubt, that Jesus did rise from the grave on that Easter Sunday morning?" I believe that the answer to this second question, and thus also to the first question, is a resounding "yes." Having made this assertion, it is only proper that I lay out for you some of the evidence. While books have been written on the resurrection of Jesus, my purpose here is not to give you an exhaustive explanation, rather a brief summary of some of the evidence for His resurrection.

Let's start with a look at one of the most influential men of history, the Apostle Paul. Paraphrasing part of I Corinthians 15, Paul wrote, "We know that Jesus Christ rose from the dead. How do we know this? Because over 500 people saw him alive at one time (after He was crucified and put in a tomb), and many of those people are yet alive with us to this day." This passage, and others from Paul's letters which became part of the New Testament and the historical records about Paul found in the book of Acts, clearly reveal some irrefutable truths that have a bearing on the question, "Did Jesus really rise from the grave?" Let's take a look at them:

First: Paul was a very intelligent man and a brilliant debater.

Second: The Apostle Paul was very controversial and had many critics who would do anything they could to discredit him. Some even wanted to kill him.

Third: The Apostle Paul was not writing with us in mind (who live nearly 2,000 years after his death); rather he was first and foremost writing to the people of his day.

Fourth: The writings of the Apostle Paul clearly establish two important things that must be considered:

One, What Paul believed.

Two, Certain things the people Paul was writing to believed.

It is obvious that the people to whom Paul was writing must have believed that Jesus arose from the grave. If they did not believe that more than 500 people saw Jesus alive after His crucifixion, Paul's assertion would have effectively destroyed his credibility. His critics would have used such a false statement to ridicule him. He would have been particularly vulnerable to the charge of hypocrisy. After all, in Paul's writings, he advocated a very high moral standard and spoke out strongly against dishonesty.

Such a blatant lie would have so discredited Paul that it is highly unlikely that we would know anything of his letters today. Brilliant man that he was, Paul was not about to make such a foolish statement if he did not believe it was true, and if he did not also believe that the people he was writing to believed it to be true.

Paul was not the only one who wrote based on this belief. The other writers of the New Testament; Matthew, Mark, Luke, John, Peter, James, and whoever wrote the book of Hebrews, all wrote from the belief that Jesus Christ was the Son of God who was killed by crucifixion, but three days later rose from the grave. In their writings, they all also assumed that the people they were writing to believed these same things. Like Paul, all of these men advocated a high moral standard. You may question the validity of their belief, but right or wrong, it borders on the absurd to even question whether they actually believed it.

The question we must answer is, "Where did this widespread belief come from?" Remember, these people were contemporaries of Jesus. There had been no time for a legend to evolve. Furthermore, they held to this belief even though it cost many of them dearly. They were literally "thrown to the lions!" We know they held steadfastly to this belief, because if they had not, the Church (a product of that belief) would not exist today.

The big question that must be answered is:

Where did the widespread belief, that Jesus arose from the grave, come from?

No one can seriously question whether Jesus lived. To suggest that the writings about Him were merely fiction is beyond incredulous. It is hard to even imagine that four separate authors could create a fictitious character so real that 500 people thought he actually lived during their lifetimes, that He was crucified by the Romans, and that they personally saw Him alive after He rose from the grave. Remember, they were so sure of these things that they were willing to die for the belief. To deny that He lived would make a mockery of all historical inquiry.

Having to admit that Jesus lived, but starting out with the assumption that miracles are impossible (some would describe this as blind prejudice), many scholarly skeptics have tried to go into the historical records about Jesus to remove the supernatural elements. Early in the 20th century, there were many respected scholars involved in this effort. Albert Schweitzer wrote a book about it, titled, *The Quest for the Historical Jesus.* These scholars were trying to describe Jesus as a simple teacher of righteousness who did not perform the miracles recorded in the Gospels. They assumed that the miracles were fictitious embellishments added to the records about the real Jesus.

While the efforts of skeptics to find a different Jesus from the Gospel accounts has continued to this day, it has proven to be an exercise in futility. In account after account, the removal of the miracle destroys the purpose for which it was written.

Furthermore, if they were ever successful in coming up with a reasonable alternative to the Jesus of the Gospels, their removal of the miracles would create an even bigger problem. They would not be able to reasonably deny that "this simple teacher of righteousness" believed He was the Messiah who was promised in the prophecies of the Old Testament. It is nearly as easy to establish that Jesus claimed He was the promised Messiah as it is to establish that he lived at all. After all, that is why the Jews had Him crucified.

If Jesus was merely a dynamic leader and teacher, as these skeptics propose, the logical conclusion is that He was a hypocritical liar or a delusional schizophrenic. As C.S. Lewis observed, either Jesus was who He claimed to be, the Son of God, or He was a liar or a lunatic. Jesus left us no other alternative.

Either Jesus was who He claimed to be, the Son of God, or He was a liar or a lunatic. Jesus left us no other alternative.

So, we know there once lived a man named Jesus who claimed He was the Messiah and whom most historians recognize as one of the greatest teachers and leaders in the history of the world. We also know that the records about Him attribute to him the supernatural power to perform miracles. And, most amazing of all, many of his contemporaries believed that three days after He died on the cross, He rose from the grave.

It is an undeniable fact that over 500 people believed they saw Jesus alive after His dead body was placed in a tomb, and many of these people believed this so strongly that they committed their lives to proclaiming this belief -- even if it meant they would die for doing so. We need to ask, "Where did this belief come from?" Skeptics have tried to explain it away by various theories. Let's take a look at them.

The first theory is that **Jesus did not really die. This is sometimes called the "swoon theory."** It suggests that after spending a day hanging on a cross, and having a spear thrust in his side, that Jesus did not really die. He merely went into a coma, was wrapped in linen and ointment and laid in a tomb. But, after three days in the tomb (without food or water) he was resuscitated, busted out of the linen and ointment that bound Him, pushed back the gigantic boulder that sealed the entrance to the tomb, and walked by the sleeping guards (who, according to Roman law, would be executed if they went to sleep on the job). In His weakened state, He then appeared to His disciples and about 500 other people before He disappeared, never to be seen or heard from again. This theory has few advocates. It is not reasonable that anyone would believe that someone in such a weakened condition was the risen Son of God.

The second theory is called: **The visionary hypothesis.** This theory suggests that the disciples did not really see Jesus alive after He was crucified and His body was placed in a tomb. They just thought they saw Him. Now, we might accept one or two visions. But over 500 people, all having the same vision, is hard to believe, unless there was something that would have psychologically encouraged them to have the visions. If Jesus had healed the sick, given sight to the blind, hearing to the deaf, and made the lame to walk, we could understand why they might have had visions. But, if He did those things, it is not hard to believe that He arose from the grave. Those miracles would substantiate His claim that He was the Messiah and the Son of God. Another major problem with this theory is that the Jews and Romans could have easily eliminated a major problem, the belief that Jesus arose, by merely going to the tomb and producing his body.

The third and most widespread explanation is: **The stolen body theory**. Recognizing that His tomb was empty, this theory alleges that someone stole the body of Jesus. But, we must ask, "Why would someone steal a decaying corpse?" Sure, the Jews had a good motive. They could have used the body to quickly squash this "new sect" that so irritated them. But, they could not produce His body to discredit the disciples who claimed that He had risen from the grave.

How about a group of Romans? You say, "Maybe they stole His body." But, why would they steal the body? What was its value? Sure, they could have sold it to the Jews. But, as we saw above, the Jews apparently could not produce His body. Furthermore, it was in the best interests of the Romans to maintain law and order. Pontius Pilate, the governor appointed by the Romans, was very much a political animal. He had to report to Caesar, and Caesar did not look kindly on turmoil or insurrections in his provinces. A missing body was certainly not in Pilate's best interest. That's why he had Roman guards posted at the tomb.

Some suggest, "The obvious explanation is that some disciples of Jesus stole His body so they could start a new religion." The problem with this theory is that they would have known that the faith they were promoting was fraudulent. But, 11 of the 12 disciples, and many of His other followers, gave their lives for the belief that Jesus rose from the grave and that He was the Messiah, the Son of God.

The records indicate that the disciples disassociated themselves from Jesus when He was on trial. That was normal, natural behavior. Peter's denial of Jesus (three times, two in response to young girls) was what we would expect of a man who was running scared. This same Peter, only a few days later, boldly risked being stoned by standing on the corner in Jerusalem, pointing his finger at the Jews and accusing them of killing their Messiah! That Peter risked his life, for no earthly gain, was unreal apart from having seen the risen Christ.

Thomas, who first doubted and said that he would not believe in the resurrection of Jesus unless he could put his finger in His nail pierced hands, was very real and human. But, the Thomas who went all the way to India as a missionary and died as a martyr was unreal apart from having later become convinced that Jesus rose from the grave and that He is the Messiah. The Bible explained that Thomas changed his mind because he met his risen Lord and Savior.

Furthermore, we have to ask, "Why would His followers think that anyone would fall for the story that Jesus was the Messiah?" Again, if Jesus actually healed the sick, gave sight to the blind, hearing to the deaf, made the lame to walk, stilled a storm, and walked on water, we can understand why they might think that people could be fooled into thinking that He was the

Messiah. But, those things would clearly establish that His claims were true and that Jesus is the Messiah, the Son of God, and thus it would be reasonable to expect that He had arisen from the grave.

When the facts are honestly considered: The alternative theories are not reasonable.

None of these alternative theories make any sense when one honestly considers the known facts. The most reasonable explanation for the historical evidence is that Jesus really was the Son of God and that He did rise from the grave on that first Easter Sunday morning.

There is an additional body of evidence that Jesus rose from the grave that is easy for us to check out today. The Bible not only tells us that Jesus rose from the grave, but Luke, chapter 24:13-32, also tells us that after he arose, he walked and talked with some men on a road to a small town called Emmaus, a few miles from Jerusalem. It also tells us what He said to them. At first these men did not recognize Jesus when He walked up along side of them. They were troubled about the things that had happened in Jerusalem, about Jesus being crucified. Jesus responded to them by saying:

> **Oh, foolish men and slow of heart to believe all that the prophets have spoken! Was it not necessary for the Christ (a word that means Messiah) to suffer these things and to enter into His glory?**

The author, Luke, continued:

> **And beginning with Moses and all of the Prophets, He explained to them in all of the Scriptures the things concerning Himself.**

This is a very significant account. In a nutshell, this record tells us that Jesus Christ claimed that the Old Testament, a book written by about 50 men over a span of nearly 1,000 years, and completed over 200 years before He was born, talked specifically about Himself when it foretold of the promised Messiah.

There is no debate as to whether the Old Testament was written before Jesus was born -- it was even translated from Hebrew to Greek about 150 years before He was born. (It is believed to be the first book ever translated from one language to another.) We have copies of that translation today, it is called the Septuagint (often written LXX -- it was translated by a team of seventy men). Consequently, using the Old Testament Scriptures, we can check out these claims by examining the biblical documents.

The evidence that Jesus rose from the grave is compelling, and His words on the road to Emmaus can be examined. If He did rise from the grave, and He is the Messiah promised in the Old Testament, then your eternal destination depends on how you respond to the truths proclaimed in the Bible. There is too much at stake for you to ignore this evidence.

If Jesus rose from the grave, and His words on the road to Emmaus are true, then your eternal destination depends upon your response to the truths proclaimed in the Bible.

I have written a book (if you are sharing this with others, you can say, "There is a book"), titled *The Master Plot of the Bible,* that explains the foundation for the Messianic promises that were written by Moses, and then examines the Old Testament Prophets and their expectations for a coming Messiah -- expectations that point to Jesus Christ. This book is only 180 pages long and can be easily read in six or seven hours.

If you have doubts about the validity of the Christian faith, the time you invest in reading this book may turn out to be the most valuable hours of your life. It will be time that will help you learn how to obtain eternal life?, (I usually add, "the plot" is not mine, and it is not a new discovery. I have merely tried to explain foundational and significant portions of the Bible in a concise format that is easy to understand.) Let me challenge you to read it. (I suggest that you loan a copy to them and later prod them by asking how they are coming with it.)

Let's review a bit before we move on to the next chapter.

1. I start with the Apostle Paul and establish that he believed that 500 people, who were still living when he wrote, believed that they had seen the living Jesus after his crucifixion and that all of the other writers of the New Testament believed in a supernatural, resurrected Jesus and were willing to die for the belief.

2. I then look at the alternative theories that have been proposed by skeptics as to where this belief came from (the swoon theory, the visionary hypothesis, and the stolen body theory) and showed their obvious absurdity.

3. I then challenge them to examine the claims Jesus made on the Road to Emmaus.

The flow of this presentation logically leads to the next major body of evidence, the evidence from fulfilled prophecy. We will look at it in the next two chapters. But remember, **"As you are going ..."** you can use the evidence for the resurrection of Jesus to help **"Make Disciples."**

Chapter Twelve

Prepared for Prophecy

For the prophecy came not in old times by the will of man; but holy men of God spoke as they were moved by the Holy Spirit.

2 Peter 1:21

The week after we took our Campus Crusade for Christ staff to invade the University of California at Berkeley (Chapter One), we moved on for a week at UCLA. Billy Graham went with us, but Holy Hubert stayed back in Berkeley.

We opened the week with Billy Graham speaking in Pauley Pavilion where the Bruins play basketball. To inform the UCLA students, we placed a full-page ad in the school paper announcing Billy's visit to the campus and that he would be speaking Monday at noon. But *The Daily Bruin* was controlled by a group of Jewish students and they "accidentally" forgot to put our full-page advertisement in the Monday issue.

We only learned that the ad did not run a few hours before Billy was scheduled to speak. Not having the benefit of the advertisement, our only alternative was to pair up, with one of us on one side of a campus street and the other on the opposite side, and to yell back and forth, "Hey, are you going to hear Billy Graham speak at Pauley Pavilion at noon today?" The answer was, "Yes, I'll see you there. I wouldn't want to miss hearing Billy Graham speak at Pauley Pavilion today at noon."

Part of the intense antagonism from the Jewish student journalists was probably because Hal Lindsey was the Campus Director for our ministry at UCLA. Hal was a student of Bible prophecy, and was he very aggressive in evangelizing the Jewish students in their fraternities and sororities.

Hal wanted the Christian students at UCLA, who were active with Campus Crusade, to profit from the week. So, he paired them up with staff members and asked them to make witnessing appointments for us and tag along as observers. I was paired with a freshman who was a new believer. He had come to know Jesus as his Savior and Messiah after Hal had spoken to a group in his Jewish fraternity.

This young believer made an appointment for me to meet with a couple of upperclassmen from his fraternity. One was a philosophy major, and they were both very skeptical about the claims of Christ. We spent over three hours together one afternoon in a coffee shop at the UCLA student union.

After explaining the Gospel, I shared with them evidence for the resurrection of Jesus. I was somewhat more detailed than the presentation in the last chapter, as these students were diligently looking for any loophole they could find.

Finally, I asked them if there were any presuppositions to the evidence I had shared with them that they could not accept, or if they could they come up with any other reasonable explanation for the evidence apart from Jesus actually having risen from the grave. They had to admit that they could not challenge the presuppositions and had no alternative explanations.

To prepare them for the evidence from fulfilled prophecy, I begin with a parable. It was my adaptation of an illustration I had read in a booklet published many years ago by InterVarsity Christian Fellowship (I don't recall the title or the author).

The new believer was sitting to my left, and his fraternity brothers were sitting across the table and on my right. I said to them, "Let's assume that we are on the top of this table, and it is impossible for us to get underneath the table. Using the assumptions of modern naturalism, the only things that exist are those things we can observe with our physical senses, so we must assume that there is no such thing as underneath the table."

"We decide to try a scientific experiment. Using the Scientific method, we come up with a hypothesis that 'Steel balls don't move unless there is a force exerted on them.' And, of course, we know that the only forces are above the table, because there is no such thing as underneath the table."

"For many years, we test the hypothesis. Anytime we use a force on a ball, it moves. Anytime there is no force, the ball does not move. After ten years of testing, we finally come up with a scientific law, 'A steel ball will not move without a force being exerted on it.'"

"Then, one time, someone comes along under the table with a magnet, and the ball moves." I asked, "What is going to happen?" Before they could reply, I answered my own question. " Well, for the next ten years, the people on top of the table will debate as to what the force was above the table that made the ball move. Two thousand years later, sophisticated people will say, 'Back in those days, they believed in fairy tales. But we know today that the ball never really moved at all!'"

"For the sake of this illustration," I continued, "let's assume that this person under the table wanted the people above the table to know about himself. So, he puts a spokesman on top of the table. We'll call him a prophet. And, the prophet says, 'So that you will know about the person under the table, at an exact time, with no force exerted on it, this ball is going to move forward, to the left, forward, to the right, and forward.' Now, you are above the table watching. The ball is in a vacuum, so you know there is no force on the ball above the table, and at the exact time foretold by the prophet, the ball moves forward, to the left, forward, to the right, and forward."

I turned to the student sitting to my right and asked, "What would you think?" I will never forget his answer. He blurted out, "I would not believe it moved!" His friend across the table looked at him with astonishment on his face and said, "I can't believe what you just said." He defended himself by saying, "I just said that I would not believe the ball moved." His friend responded, "No you didn't. You just said, 'I am a closed minded bigot.'" At that, the new believer to my left almost fell off of his chair laughing.

My purpose in sharing this illustration with those students was to overcome a misconception about Bible prophecy. When you mention Bible prophecy to skeptics, they often assume that you are looking at vague generalities and good guesses that just happened to have come true. Their thinking is often influenced by the so called "modern day prophets" who base their supposed prophecies on trends of the times they live in, or merely make a lot of guesses hoping that a few will happen, thus giving them credibility.

The Old Testament test for prophets required 100% accuracy. Failure to meet this standard brought on death by stoning.

The Old Testament had a much higher standard than that demanded by the grocery store tabloids. It demanded 100% accuracy, and the penalty for failure to pass that test was death (Deuteronomy 19:18-22). If we still had that standard and penalty, I am sure we would have fewer people claiming to be prophets.

In recent years, I came up with another illustration that really communicates to sports fans. As a graduate of the University of Oregon and remembering our rivalry with Oregon State University, in my book *The Master Plot of the Bible*, I word it as follows in the first printing of the book:

"Let me explain the difference between a prediction and a prophecy. With a prediction I see "this and this," and I therefore predict 'that' will happen." (I usually point with my finger first to the right and then way to the left as I am saying this.) "If it comes true, it would be a good prediction.

But, a prophecy does not look at factors that might cause it to happen. For example, as an Oregon Duck, I illustrated this in my first printing of my book, *The Master plot of the Bible*, by saying, 'If you looked at all of the good football players that Florida State University has recruited and said, "They are going to win a national championship,' and it happened, that would be a good prediction. But if you said, 'Oregon State University is going to win a national championship in football,' and it happened, that would be a phenomenal prophecy!"

When I witness to Texans, having lived in College Station for many years and having become an Aggie fan, I use Texas A&M and Rice in the above example.

Recently, during basketball season when everyone was predicting Duke would be an easy winner at the Final Four, I contrasted Duke University winning the national championship in basketball versus Duke winning a national championship in football. Then UConn beat Duke in the finals and my first reaction was to assume that it ruined my illustration. On further reflection, I realized that it illustrates the problem an imposter prophet would face when confronted with the Old Testament test of 100% accuracy. It makes the accuracy of the biblical prophecies even more significant.

Feel free to use this illustration and change the parties to communicate to the people you are sharing with. That way, it can become "your illustration." I hope to get *The Master Plot of the Bible,* translated into Spanish. If I do, I will use Brazil and the United States in predictions for the soccer championship at the World Cup. If you are witnessing to a Frenchman, I would suggest that Brazil be replaced with France. When Dennis Erickson became the football coach at Oregon State, and they started winning, I changed this illustration to the Duke basketball and Duke Football teams in the second printing of *The Master Plot of the Bible* -- to be sure it remained strong.

An understanding of context greatly increases one's comprehension.

It has been said, "Without an understanding of context, nothing has any meaning." This may be somewhat of a stretch, but there is no doubt that an understanding of context is often crucial when examining the validity of an assertion. I believe that this is pertinent when presenting the prophetic evidence that shows that Jesus is the Messiah, whom God sent to Israel to provide blessings for the whole world.

It is often assumed that the key to effectively present Bible prophecy is to show ***how many prophecies point to Jesus Christ.***

It is my belief that an often unanswered, but more vital, question is, ***"Why are these prophecies in the Bible?"*** This is where an understanding of context is important. I believe that a short explanation of context greatly strengthens the impact of the messianic prophecies that point to Jesus.

In chapter one of *The Master Plot of the Bible*, I explain that one must grasp both the immediate and broad the context of scriptural passages. To answer the "why" question, it is important that the broad context of the Bible be briefly explained.

As you will see in the next chapter, my presentation of Bible prophecy begins with a short explanation of why God chose a single nation, Israel, as a channel through whom He could bless all families of the world, and how He promised to provide those blessings through a Messiah-Redeemer. When these truths are explained, the stage is set, and the prophecies become much more significant and believable.

If I know that I will have adequate time, I always preface my presentation of prophecy with the two clarifications discussed in this chapter. First, I use a prediction illustration from the sports world, them, as I begin my presentation about prophecy, I set the stage by explaining its purpose. The focus of my presentation is on both the nation of Israel and the promises for a Messiah pointing to Jesus.

My presentation of prophecy is in the next chapter of this book. It is also in letter form in my Witnessing Letters packet. Just as with the evidence for the ressurection, sometime the most effective way to present this evidence is to ask someone to read the letter and ask them to "tell me what you think of it." If you don't yet have a set of the Witnessing Letters, you can get them at a Christian bookstore (ISBN 0-9657835-3-7). While the letters are copyrighted, permission is granted to make unaltered copies.

So, be prepared and remember, **"as you are going..."** one of the most powerful tools at your disposal is the evidence from fulfilled biblical prophecies. Use it to help **"make disciples!"**

Chapter Thirteen
Jesus is the Promised Messiah

... and His name shall be called Wonderful, Counselor, The Mighty God, The Everlasting Father, The Prince of Peace.
Isaiah 9:6

What did Jesus, Peter, Stephen, Philip, Barnabas, Apollos, the Apostle Paul, and probably many others in the early church have in common when they witnessed for Jesus? The answer: They reasoned from the Old Testament to convince people that Jesus was the promised Messiah. Look at Paul and Apollos as examples.

Dr. Luke wrote that Apollos "... powerfully refuted the Jews in public, demonstrating by the Scriptures the Jesus was the Christ *(the Messiah)*" (Acts 18:28).

Luke also wrote, in the closing days of Paul's life he was "... trying to persuade them concerning Jesus from both the Law of Moses and from the Prophets from morning until evening" (Acts 28:23).

Just as Jesus, on the road to Emmaus (Luke 24:27), began with Moses, so also, Paul started his discourses from the writings of Moses. I think that there is a very important lesson to be learned from their examples.

It is my observation, when skeptics try to read the Bible, most do not understand why there is so much emphasis on Israel. Some think, "I am not a Jew, so why should I be concerned about what I believe was their "tribal god." Others merely ask, "Why all the talk about Israel?"

I recommend that you begin your presentation of the Messianic prophecies from the writings of Moses, because from Moses we can learn the answer to the questions, "Why Israel?" and "Why a Messiah?"

In brief, the stage is set in Genesis where it tells us that man rebelled, became sinful, and was separated from God. Genesis then lays a foundation for God's progressive revelation of His solution for man's sin problem. When God made His covenant promise to Abraham (and repeated it to Isaac and Jacob), He clearly said that they were chosen to be vessels through whom "all families of the world will be blessed" (Genesis 12:13, 26:4, and 28:14). As the Bible's message unfolds, we learn further that these blessings will come through a descendant of King David. This one, who will sit on David's throne, will be the Messiah-King, our redeemer. The prophecies about the promised Messiah clearly point to the King of Kings, Jesus Christ.

The Bible tells us that God selected the descendants of Abraham, who became the nation of Israel, to be the channel through whom He could provide blessings for all families of the earth.

I always try to preface the fulfilled prophecies, that point to Jesus as the Jewish Messiah, by preparing the way with a short introduction of how God choose one nation, Israel, to provide a channel through whom He could provide blessings for all families of the world. I then explain how the Old Testament provides the "roots" for the redemption that God gave us through Jesus, the Messiah, who was a descendant of Abraham, Isaac, Jacob, and King David.

A fuller treatment of this material can be found in my book *The Master Plot of the Bible* and I encourage you to read it in preparation for presenting Bible prophecy. But, however you do it, be sure to use the powerful evidence from the Old Testament that clearly establishes that Jesus is the promised Messiah.

As with the evidence for the resurrection, you can also find this same presentation in letter-form (yes, you can make copies) in the packet I call *Witnessing Letters.* ISBN 0-9657835-3-

7 at Christian bookstores. Though I have made this presentation verbally, many times, I now prefer to ask someone to read the letter, rather than listen to me present it orally. The printed page seems to give it more power.

The rest of this chapter is how I present this powerful evidence. Again, I encourage you to use this presentation in any way. Do notice that it has a logical progression. Also notice that I do not always give the exact verse reference (because of time constraints). I do usually give the name of the prophet who gave us the prophecy, and if they ask, I will open my Bible and show it to them. (Notice that when Peter and Paul presented Old Testament truth in the book of Acts, they quoted scripture without giving an exact reference). Again, God's word is a sword that does not need to be proven, just used.

There are parts of this presentation that we have already explained in this book. Rather than eliminating it, it is repeated so that you can see how I use it in the context of a presentation. With this background, let's look at my presentation:

A king once asked his chaplain for one piece of evidence for the inspiration of the Bible. The chaplain pointed across the room and replied, "There is the evidence, the Jew, your majesty." When the chaplain pointed to a Jew, he was referring the king to the amazing prophecies in the Bible about the people of one nation, Israel.

This story raises some issues that I would like to clarify. First, what is meant the word *inspiration;* second, what is meant by the word *prophecy;* third, *how and why* does the Bible have prophecies; and finally, why does the Bible focus so much on the people from one nation, the Israelites.

The New Testament Greek word translated "inspiration" is a two-part word that means, "God breathed." This concept was expressed by Peter when he wrote, **"For the prophecy came not in old time by the will of man: but holy men of God spoke as they were moved by the Holy Spirit"** (2 Peter 1:21).

There is a big difference between predictions made in our time and biblical prophecies. Let me illustrate it for you. If someone looked at all of the great basketball players at Duke

University and foretold that Duke would win a national championship, and it happened, that would be a good prediction based on a perceptive observation.

On the other hand, if someone foretold that Duke would win a national championship in football, and it happened, that would be a phenomenal prophecy. The obvious difference is that our predictions are educated guesses while biblical prophecies foretold things that were, at best, highly improbable. Even more improbable than a Duke University football team winning a national championship.

Bible prophecies are not guesses based on probability. Rather, they foretell future events and details that are often highly improbable.

In Deuteronomy chapter 18, Moses explained the *how and why.* He wrote that God would put His words in the mouths of His prophets. He warned potential impostor prophets that they would face the death penalty for their false prophecies. But, the fulfillment of the prophecies that God gave through His prophets would verify that they were speaking **"the thing that the Lord has spoken."** In other words, God's message to mankind in the Bible was so important that God left His indelible fingerprints on its pages, so that we can know that it is from Him.

The Bible teaches that man was originally in close fellowship with God, but this fellowship with God was broken as the result of man exercising his free will in an act of sinful disobedience. The result of this sin was spiritual separation from God. But God, still desiring an object of His love, determined that He would work in the history of the human race to restore the broken fellowship.

To expedite His plan of redemption, God chose Abram (whom He later renamed Abraham). God's stated purpose, when He chose Abraham, was that He wanted to use him and his descendants as a channel through whom he could bring blessings to all families of the world.

As part of His plan, God promised to give his descendants some land. While Abraham had other descendants, the Bible tells us that God's promise of the land and blessings were to flow through his son Isaac and his grandson Jacob. Jacob, whom God renamed Israel, had twelve sons, and their descendants became known as the children of Israel or the twelve tribes of Israel. These tribes ultimately became a nation. One of the tribes was named Judah, and members of that tribe were called Jews. Sometimes the name Jews encompasses those from all twelve tribes.

The Old Testament history of the Israelites tells of the development of God's plan. As the result of a famine, Israel and his family migrated to Egypt where they multiplied and became slaves. After 430 years in Egypt (400 as slaves), God raised up a deliverer named Moses. God worked through Moses in a supernatural way to get the Egyptians to release their slaves (yes, supernatural; after all, He is God).

After they left Egypt, Moses led the Israelites to Mount Sinai. At Mount Sinai, God gave them a promise and instructions (some call these instructions their constitution). Through Moses, God promised the Israelites that if they were obedient to His instructions, He would "... make you a kingdom of priests, a holy nation."

Since the Israelites accepted and agreed to follow God's instructions, God gave them some warnings through Moses, as they were about to enter into "the promised land." He promised to bless them if they were obedient, but He warned of curses that would come upon them if they were disobedient.

The Bible foretold that if Israel were disobedient they would be scattered all over the world, suffer persecution, but eventually they would be returned to their land.

Through Moses, God warned the Israelites that their disobedience would lead to their being taken captive to a heathen nation, that a second nation, whose language they would not understand, would later attack them and destroy their city, and that they would be scattered as a people among all the nations of the world where they would suffer extreme persecution. After giving them these warnings, Moses assured them that there would be a time when God would purify their hearts and regather them back to the Promised Land.

The Old Testament was written by Israelites, but it was not a propaganda piece. It records that they did not follow the instructions God gave through Moses, that they were disobedient. Consequently, Moses' warnings became prophecies that have been fulfilled so precisely that they became pre-recorded history.

Several generations after they entered the Promised Land, the Israelites asked God to give them a king. The first king He gave them was Saul. But Saul was disobedient, and the kingship was removed from him and given to another, King David. David was a great conquering king.

After subduing the nations around them, David decided that he would build a house for God. But, God sent David a message, through the prophet Nathan, that David was not to be the one who would build a house (a temple) for Him. God promised that David's son, who would follow him as king, would build a temple for God. And he promised that the kingship would never be removed from David's descendants as it had been from Saul's. God further promised that David's house, throne, and kingdom would endure forever.

Through His prophets, God foretold that the Messiah-Redeemer would be a descendant of King David.

When David was made king, his head was anointed with oil. The Old Testament prophets foretold of a future king who would be a descendant of David. This future king was referred to as "The Anointed One," or as translated today, "The Messiah."

During the reigns of the Israelite kings, God used His prophets as His spokesmen to the nation. They exhorted the Israelites to holy living and in some cases foretold what God would do in the future. God's message, given through the prophets, repeatedly focused on five main points: 1. They pointed out the sins of the people and the nation; 2. They called on the children of Israel to repent and return to the original law (the constitution that God had given through Moses); 3. They warned of divine judgment to come upon them if they did not repent and follow the Law; 4. They reasserted God's eternal promise that there would be a descendant of Abraham who would sit on David's throne; 5. They foretold of future blessings for Israel, and for all families of the world, that would be ushered in when their Messiah reigns as King.

In these future blessings, the prophets often proclaimed two main themes: A King is coming, and He will establish His righteous rule on earth from Jerusalem. Interwoven with these themes, God's prophets foretold that when the Messiah-King sits on the throne of David, the Israelites will be regathered from all the nations where they had been scattered, and they will occupy the Promised Land and live in peace.

God's prophets foretold many details about the promised Messiah. Isaiah repeatedly referred to Him as **"the Holy One of Israel"** who would be born of a virgin and be called Immanuel (which means "God with us"). Micah foretold that His birth would take place in a small town called Bethlehem. Isaiah also wrote **"... a child will be born to us, a son will be given to us ... and He will be called Wonderful, Counselor, Mighty God, Eternal Father, Prince of Peace..."**

But Isaiah also wrote that he would be a descendant of Jesse, King David's father. What amazing prophecies. The promised Messiah was to be born in Bethlehem of a virgin woman, be a descendant of King David, and yet be referred to as God, a Son who was given.

The prophet Isaiah also gave details as to why the promised Messiah would be sent. He explained that **"All we like sheep have gone astray, we have turned each one to his own way, but the Lord has laid on Him the sin of us all"** ... that **"He**

poured out His soul an offering for sin," and that **"My righteous servant will justify many and He will bear their iniquities** (their sin)." (There are more details in Isaiah chapter 53.)

The prophet Zechariah foretold that the Messiah would present himself to the nation on the back of a donkey. Talk about an improbable prophecy. An imposter prophet might have predicted that the greatest King in the history of the world would be presented on a dashing white charger, but not on a donkey.

The prophet Daniel even prophesied when the Messiah would present Himself. The beginning and ending dates of this amazing prophecy can be confirmed within one year by the dates of the reigns of two ancient rulers (Artaxerxes and Tiberius Caesar). Both dates are found in the biographical section of a Webster's Dictionary or an encyclopedia. (The math is explained in Chapter seven of *The Master Plot of the Bible* and in many other books on Bible prophecy.)

A psalmist described in great detail His death. Centuries before the Romans began the use of crucifixion in Israel, it was written that someone would pierce His hands and feet, divide His garments among them, and cast lots for His outer robe.

Ezekiel foretold that the Messiah would enter Jerusalem through the Golden Gate on the East side of the city, but that sometime after He entered by it, that Gate would be sealed shut. When Jesus presented Himself as Messiah on the back of a donkey, on the original Palm Sunday, He entered the Jerusalem through that gate. Today there is a masonry wall within the ancient arch of the Golden Gate that stands as solid rock evidence that the Messiah has already entered Jerusalem.

The Old Testament Prophecies about the Messiah seem to be contradictory.

It has been noted that the Messianic prophecies seem to have a major contradiction. Some passages describe the coming Messiah as a humble servant who would be despised and rejected of men and even be cut off from His people. Other passages describe Him as a powerful ruling King who will establish His righteous rule over the earth. Some ancient rabbis even speculated that there might be two Messiahs.

After the Old Testament was completed, four hundred years passed by and a baby was born in Bethlehem who divided history into B.C. and A.D. The records about this descendant of Abraham and David, named Jesus, tell us He healed the sick, gave sight to the blind, hearing to the deaf and that He performed many other miracles.

We know that He was rejected by His own people (this had also been foretold), was nailed by His hands and feet to a cross, and died of crucifixion. Then, an amazing thing happened. Three days later His tomb was empty, and He personally appeared to His followers before He ascended to be with His Father in Heaven. Before He departed, He promised that sometime He would return to earth.

The contradiction disappears when we understand that they described one Messiah who would come two different times.

The Old Testament prophets were not speaking of two Messiahs, rather of one Messiah who would come two different times. Jesus, the Messiah, first came as the humble servant who died on the cross as a sacrifice for our sin, but He promised He will return in power and great glory to establish His righteous kingdom.

When Jesus spoke of His future return, He said that no one would know its exact time. However, He did say that there would be signs that would indicate that the time of His return was near. Consistent with the Old Testament prophecies, Jesus said that when He finally returns to earth, Jerusalem will again be occupied and controlled by the Jews. But in the mean time, **"Jerusalem will be trampled down by the Gentiles** (non-Jews) **until the time of the Gentiles be fulfilled."**

For centuries, skeptics scoffed at the Bible's prophecies that the Holy Land would again be occupied and controlled by a regathered nation of Israel. They asserted that it was not only improbable; it was also politically and militarily impossible. From a human perspective, they were right.

In 1948, when David Ben Gurion declared Israel an independent state on a small parcel of land, the Arab nations quickly attacked and announced that they were going to annihilate all of the Jews in Palestine. The Arabs had a 650,000-man fighting force that were equipped with the best weapons and air power that oil money could buy. The Israelites had a 45,000-man defense force, weapons for only 2 out of 3 of them, a three days' supply of ammunition, and some unarmed Piper Cubs (during the war, some Jews from Europe flew in some old German fighter planes).

When the war ended, the Jews were not merely survivors, they had greatly expanded their territory and had even captured half of Jerusalem. Later in the Six Day War of 1967, the Jews gained control of the rest of the Holy City. Many Bible scholars believe that this has set the stage for "the final chapter."

The prophet Zechariah foretold what will happen when the Messiah finally presents Himself to Israel. He describes a time when **"God will whistle"** for the Israelites and the scattered people will return to the Promised Land. He also describes a siege of Jerusalem that will take place at that time in which all of the nations of the world will attack Israel. But Zechariah 12:10 tells us that their Messiah will defend them, and they (the Jews) will then **"look on Me whom they have pierced."** Let me ask you, "Who did the Jews pierce?" *(If they respond, Jesus, I say,* "That's right." *(If they don't, I supply the answer.)*

I then conclude, "I believe the evidence from the messianic prophecies establishes, beyond any reasonable doubt, that Jesus is the Messiah, promised in the Old Testament."

If they continue to question, I often say, "I have had several people respond to this information by saying, 'But, it's all too improbable. You may also feel that way. But, you need to remember that probability is affected by purpose. There are thousands of houses in this city, and if purpose is not considered, it is very improbable that I will go to any particular house after work. But if I am hungry, probability is not relevant. I am going home where some food is waiting for me on the table."

Probability is irrelevant when someone has a purpose.

I continue, "Always remember, God had a purpose when He spoke through the Old Testament prophets. He wanted us to know, without a doubt, that when He sent His son Jesus, we would know that He is **'the Lamb of God,'** who was offered on the cross to pay the price for our sin. And, that makes it a very important truth, wouldn't you agree?"

Notice that at the end, I Again bring it back to the central truth, that God gave us prophecies so that we would know that Jesus is the Messiah, our Savior. That is the most important truth I want them to remember. Remember, to get the full impact of this scriptural truth, you need to first be sure that they understand the message of the cross.

As mentioned previously, the above is in letter form (that can be duplicated) in the Witnessing Letters packet. (The letters do include verse references.) You can also encourage your skeptical friends to read a more complete presentation of this material in *The Master Plot of the Bible.*

Just as Peter and Paul asked people to respond, and to place their faith in Jesus after prophetic truth was presented, so also, we need to ask for commitments today. Our goal is not merely to inform people. We need to remember that their eternal destiny is at stake and encourage them to step out in faith and receive Jesus as their Savior.

This life will soon pass for all of us. I do hope that when I get to Heaven I will meet people who became disciples as a result of your having shared with them, **"as you were going,"** the evidence that Jesus is the Messiah. What a time it will be as we all rejoice together.

Chapter Fourteen

If they have never heard

How shall they call on Him in whom they have not believed? and how shall they believe in Him of whom they have not heard? and how shall they hear without a preacher?

Romans 10:14

Christians believe that faith in Jesus Christ is the only way for one to get to Heaven. But, it is often asked, "Isn't that just bigotry? After all, what about all the people of other religions, and what about the people in the world who have never heard of Jesus?" A common expression of this last question is, "What about the natives in Africa who have never heard?" I understand that in Africa the question is different. Over there, some ask, "What about the heathen in America who have never heard?"

The people you share Christ with may not consider themselves "heathen," but when you witness to someone, you better be prepared for questions about people of other religions and the people who have never heard about Jesus.

Unless you are called to minister to a particular group of a different religion, I don't think that you need to be an expert on other religions to deal with this issue. The strategy in this chapter is not intended to reach someone who is committed to another religion. Rather, it is an approach I have found effective when dealing with the average American who couldn't care less about the other religions of the world, but use this issue as intellectual justification for their rejection of Christianity.

For me, to pose as an expert on world religions would only reveal my ignorance. But, when I am witnessing to an avowed skeptic, I welcome this issue, because it gives me an opportunity to clarify the message of God's grace by contrasting it to *man's works.*

It is often easier to explain what you believe by contrasting it with what you do not believe. The general teaching of the religions of the world is salvation by works. As a matter of fact, salvation by works is nearly a universal view of mankind. Contrasting works and grace is a good way to clarify why Jesus is the only way one can spend eternity with God.

Contrasting salvation by good works with salvation by grace explains why Jesus is the only way and might also clarify the Gospel.

The following explanation will not satisfy everyone. But for some, this information will help them understand the rationale for the Christian belief that Jesus is the only way to heaven, and also help them better understand the truth of the Gospel.

When approaching this issue, I admit that the Bible is dogmatic and if Jesus is not the only way to Heaven, then I am a bigot (this eliminates the necessity to defend myself against this charge). Furthermore, I admit that if it is not true, then I am a follower of the biggest bigot in all of history. After all, Jesus claimed, **"I am the way, the truth, and the life, no one can come to the Father** (God) **except through Me"** (John 14:6).

"On the other hand," I explain, "I have another book that is just as dogmatic as my Bible. It's the Owner's Manual for my car. It says that the only fuel I can put in my car's tank is gasoline. The authors of that book are so bigoted that they say my car will not run on water or milk. Furthermore, they specify that I need a particular grade of motor oil in the crankcase. Vinegar is a great cleanser, but my Owner's Manual dogmatically says I can't substitute it for oil."

Some will respond, "But the Owner's Manual for your car was written by the engineers who designed your car." (If they don't, then I say it for them.) My response is that the Bible claims that God, who designed us, spoke through the writers of the Old and

New Testament when the Bible was written. In essence, the Bible is the "Owner's Manual" God has given us so that we can function as He intended. Continuing this analogy, I say, "But, something has gone terribly wrong, and each one of us is desperately in need of a 'valve job.' More about the *valve job* later. But first, let's look at this claim that the Bible is the one and only *Owner's Manual God has given us."*

All of the religions of the world are either natural religions or revealed religions.

I explain: While I am not an expert on the religions of the world, I do know that the religions of the world can be broadly divided into two groups: those that claim to be *revealed religions* and those that do not. Those in the latter group are often called *natural religions.*

There are only three major religions in the world that even claim to be *revealed*: Judaism, Christianity, and Islam. All the rest, the *natural religions,* are human speculation based on limited knowledge. They often have valid truths -- in particular about morality. But, on the ultimate questions, they can only make guesses.

Natural religions often have some valid truths. But, on eternal questions, they can only guess.

Many of the Oriental religions believe in reincarnation. In some ways, this is an admission that they have not found adequate answers for this life. Try as one may, it seems to be impossible to live up to the moral standards that seem reasonable. So, their only hope is in a future life where one can do better.

It also seems reasonable for me to assume that if we can know anything about God, it would be because He has chosen to tell us about Himself. On the other hand, if one assumes that God has left it up to us to discover Him, one must question whether such a god would be worth discovering.

Turning to the major religions that claim to be revealed, three (Judaism, Christianity, and Islam) believe the Old Testament in the Bible is a revelation from God. The Jews recognize the Old Testament, Christianity and Islam include the Bible's New Testament, and Islam adds the Koran.

The problem with the Islamic position is that the Bible and the Koran present diametrically opposed requirements for salvation. Many years ago, an international student at Oklahoma University expressed to me his belief in the Islamic requirement to get to heaven as the following:

> In Islam, we believe you have two angels. One is on your right hand recording your good deeds. The other is on your left hand recording your bad deeds. At the judgment day they are put on the scales. If your good deeds outweigh your bad deeds, you will go to heaven. If your bad deeds outweigh your good deeds, you will go to hell, unless you died in a holy war; then you will automatically go to heaven.

His explanation of this teaching from the Koran, clearly sets it in opposition to the teachings in the Bible. Consequently, the Bible and the Koran cannot both be right.

In contrast, the Bible teaches us that God does not grade by the curve, that life is a pass or fail course and to pass, based on the life you live, you need a perfect score. Or, we could express it, "You have to live a sinless life."

Some call this "Plan A," get to heaven by living a perfect life. We all fail the test under this plan, but the Bible has good news. There is a "Plan B," accept Jesus Christ as your savior and be forgiven because He died on the cross and paid in full the price for your sin. Using the previous analogy of an automobile, accepting Jesus and being "born again" is equivalent to getting a new engine.

The difference between biblical Christianity and every other religion of the world (whether a natural religion or one that claims to be a revelation) is delineated by the difference between *works* and *grace*. Every other religion says, "You earn your standing with God based on what YOU do -- by *your* good works." When we are honest, we have to admit that having to make it by our good works is "bad news."

The Bible teaches that you can only make it to heaven **by appropriating what GOD has done <u>for you</u> through JESUS when He died on the cross and paid the penalty for your sin.** That is "good news."

I sometimes add the following to clarify this contrast by saying: "Let's compare it to two marriages. In the first marriage, the husband says, 'I want to do good things for my wife, because if I do, she will do good things for me.' And, the wife says, 'I want to do good things for my husband so that he will do good things for me.' In the second marriage, the husband says, 'I want to do good things for my wife because I love her and I want her to be happy,' and the wife says, 'I want to do good things for my husband because I love him and I want him to be happy.'"

After contrasting these two kinds of marriages, I ask, "Which marriage would be most successful?" Every person whom I have asked this question has responded, "The second marriage." I then respond, "The first marriage is a picture of man earning salvation by his good works. The second is a picture of the Bible's way. It says, **'For God so loved the world that He gave.'** I then conclude the illustration by asking, 'If the first way will not work in marriage, why should we think it would work in our relationship with God?' No one has ever given me a good answer to that question.

Some will ask, "What about the person of another religion who has never heard about Jesus?" Let me preface the following by saying that I can't be dogmatic about this, as I might be wrong. But, Jesus gave us a parable about the Pharisee and the Publican that I believe speaks to this question.

The Pharisee was a very religious man, and the Publican was an evil tax collector (they were the bad guys back then, too). Jesus said that both came to the temple at the same time. The Pharisee said, **"Thank you, God, that I am not like this miserable wretch, this Publican. I am not like other people; look at all the good things I have done."** The Publican would not even raise his head, but he prayed, **"God, be merciful to**

me a sinner." Jesus said, **"It was the Publican who went home justified and not the Pharisee."** (Luke 18:9-14 paraphrased).

From this parable, it seems to me that if someone who has never heard of Jesus goes to God and in essence prays; "God, I have blown it. I know I am guilty before you. But, I ask you for mercy, and I trust you for whatever provision you have made for my sin," they would be placing their faith in Jesus. I am never dogmatic about this explanation, but it communicates a possible solution for this problem, while again emphasizing the grace of God.

Sometimes I insert a little humor here to prepare them for the hard words that will follow. When I do, I comment:

"Oh, by the way, did you ever hear about the Sunday School teacher who taught her class about the parable of the Pharisee and the Publican? When she finished the lesson, she closed it by saying, 'Now children, let's close this class in prayer and thank the Lord that we are not like that Pharisee.'"

When I attempt to answer questions about the people who have never heard about Jesus, everything I tell them is leading up to the following, which should be shared in a remorseful spirit:

"On the other hand, while I can't be sure about my interpretation of this parable, there is another teaching from Jesus that is very clear. He said, **'To those to whom much is given, much will be required.'** On the judgment day, you will not have the excuse that you never heard the Good News about Jesus and his death on the cross for you."

"A wise man once said, 'I'm not bothered by what I don't understand in the Bible. What really concerns me is that which I do understand in the Bible.' And on the judgment day, I would rather be a native in Africa who had never heard about Jesus, than an American who had been exposed to the truth about Jesus, over and over again, but ignored it and thus rejected Him.

The Bible is very clear that God's judgment is based in part on the light that has been given ... and you have been exposed to the Good News about Jesus." And, Jesus said, **"He who is not with Me is against Me."** (Matthew 12:30 -- In a verse such as this one, you need to know the reference, but you don't need to give it to them, unless they ask.)

"The only one way we could know if God has made a provision for our sin is if He, our creator, gave us a revelation, an *Owner's Manual.* The Bible claims to be God's Owner's Manual. And ... it has 'GOOD NEWS.' The good news is that even though we are guilty, God sent His son Jesus to die on the cross as our substitute to pay in full the penalty for our sin."

"You can search the religions and philosophies of the world and apart from the cross of Jesus Christ; you will not find pardon for your sin. Only Jesus offers you release from the burden of guilt and only Jesus can give you a lasting peace and joy in your innermost being. And best of all, it is a free gift. All you have to do is accept Jesus and receive eternal life."

After sharing the above, it is often a good time to ask them if they would like to receive Jesus as their Savior. While this explanation will not satisfy everyone who asks these questions, I have found that it often satisfies the sincere questioner who is plagued by this issue.

I remember one young woman in particular. She was a student at Texas A&M, and was really bothered by this question. A friend brought her to my office, and after I shared the above with her, it was like a roadblock had been removed. She was then ready, and prayed to receive Jesus as her Savior.

Please notice the specific strategy I follow as I deal with this issue. Let's review the flow of thought that I recommend:

1. Admit that the Christian message is narrowminded and readily admit to being a bigot if it is not true. (You thus eliminate this objection.)
2. Use the owner's manual of your car illustration to demonstrate that dogmatism is not always objectionable.
3. Admit you are not an expert on religions of the world, but that you do know there are only two kinds, i.e. natural and revealed.

4. Eliminate the natural religions from consideration because the natural religions can at best make guesses, and it is not reasonable to assume that God would leave it up to us to find out about Him without His help.
5. Use Islam to contrast works and grace. (This is a very important part, as it allows you to repeat the Gospel from a different context.)
6. Give a plausible solution to the paradox by telling about the Pharisee and the Publican. (But, don't try to be dogmatic on this part.)
7. Warn them, "You will not have that excuse on the judgment day, because you have heard."

Use part of this presentation, all of it, or none of it. But **"As You are Going..."** make sure that your potential disciples understand that Jesus is the only way, because He is the only one who offers them pardon for their sin, and that they will be accountable because they have heard the message. Do that, and you will -- **Make Disciples.**

Chapter Fifteen

How About the Hypocrites?

They went out from us, but they were not of us; for if they had been of us, they would no doubt have continued with us; but they went out, that they might be made manifest that they were not all of us.

I John 2:19

Second only to the question about people of other religions and those who have never heard about Jesus, the most common objection to Christianity is the charge that the church is full of hypocrites. As with the question about those who have never heard, I look forward to people making this charge, as it gives me an opportunity to restate the message of God's grace.

A little humor always helps. When this charge is made, I like to start off by having some fun by using two quips. One I heard just recently from Chuck Colson, and the other I heard from Bob Luther when I was a new believer over thirty-five years ago.

When Chuck Colson is confronted with the charge that the Church is full of hypocrites, he responds by saying, "You're right. The Church is full of hypocrites. Come on and join us. You will fit right in and feel right at home."

Bob's quip is, "There is no doubt that the Church is full of hypocrites. But, I had to decide whether I wanted to spend an hour a week with them in Church, or eternity with them in hell." I sometimes add with a chuckle, "Hey, if you prefer spending all that time with the hypocrites, it's your decision, not mine."

On a more serious note, I suggest that they first define the term hypocrite. The obvious answer is that a hypocrite is someone who claims to be something that he/she is not. And, then I add, "You should not judge Christianity by looking at someone who merely claims to be a Christian. After all, there are people who are faking it. The person you really need to look at, and evaluate, is Jesus Christ Himself."

I continue and ask them, "Do you think that Jesus was a hypocrite?" Very few people will answer yes. If they do, I ask why they feel that way. Their reasons usually vanish, or they reveal their utter ignorance. In either case, I don't argue the point. Rather, I challenge them to read through the Gospel of John and see if they can find for me any solid evidence of hypocrisy in the life of Jesus.

When someone makes the hypocrite charge, it is usually an indication that they do not understand the Gospel message. If I have not yet explained the Gospel to them, I use the charge as a way to get into the Gospel by saying, "I understand your complaint. A lot of Christians don't practice what they preach. Real Christians don't claim to be perfect, just forgiven. If you have a few minutes, I'd like to share something with you and see if it agrees with your understanding of the Bible's picture of Christianity. Do you have a few minutes?"

Christians do not claim to be perfect -- just forgiven.

Notice what this does. It uses their criticism of Christians as a reason to get them to let you share the Gospel with them.

Some people truly believe that the Christian message is invalidated by the evidence of flagrant sin in the life of people who claim to be believers. Particularly when they hear of the sin in the lives of some Christian leaders, whether it be TV evangelists whose sins have made the national news, or a local preacher. They reason, "How could Christianity be true, if Christians do things like that?"

If there were no hypocrites in the church, it would indicate that the Bible is not true.

When such concerns are raised, I share with them, "If there were no hypocrites in the church, I would have to conclude that the Bible is not true." I explain, "The Bible does not teach that man's sin nature is removed when one becomes a Christian. Rather, God promises us victory over sin if, and only if, we walk yielded to Him. Consequently, a Christian who is not yielded to the Holy Spirit is capable of any sin that is common among the most sinful men."

I sometimes share an experience I had when I was a young man. During the summer between my second and third years of seminary, I was working with my father in the real estate business. One day I stopped by our office to pick up something. I parked in a diagonal parking space a few doors from our office, ran inside and back out a few minutes later. As I was getting into my car, I spotted a note on my windshield, picked it up and it read (in faulty English), "Do you mean to tell me that you don't do no sin? I work up at the Cupboard Cafe. Stop by tonight and argue with me about it."

I turned around, and there, sitting on a barstool in a tavern, was a woman waving at me and pointing at herself. Apparently, she had asked the bartender about me, and he told her that I was in training to be a minister.

That night, I stopped by the Cupboard Cafe and gave her a copy of an evangelistic letter put out by Campus Crusade for Christ called the Van Dusen Letter. I explained that my life was not perfect, but Christ had made some big changes in it, and suggested that she read the letter, and then she would understand what I was talking about.

A few days later, I found out that she had read the letter and had prayed to receive Jesus as her Savior. She told me she had some problems and asked me if I would counsel her. I declined, and explained that as a young single man I did not counsel single women, and referred her to a friend who was a local pastor. (She was divorced, a couple of years older than I was, and I saw potential trouble if I tried to help her.) She continued to pursue me "for counsel" over the next few weeks, and I continued to refuse and suggested she meet with my friend.

Finally, a friend of hers, who had been a foster child in my sister's home, wrote me a letter that blasted me by saying, "One thing I like is people who can help other people and they help them. One thing I don't like is people who can help other people and they won't, and that's you, Bob Prall. And, if you don't think you can control your lusts, then I think that you are a weak person."

In response to her letter, I sent her a copy of the Van Dusen Letter, explained what had happened, and concluded the letter by writing one of the wisest things I have ever written in my whole life. I wrote, "In your letter you said you think I am a weak person. Every person is weak, and I pray that God will never let me forget it."

**Every person is weak.
I pray that God never lets me forget it.**

I use this story to explain and illustrate the biblical teaching that, as fallen human beings, we are by nature sinful. That is why we all need to be forgiven through Christ's death on the cross. But, even after placing our faith in Jesus, we put ourselves in grave danger if we think that, in and of ourselves, we are strong.

I then explain, "The Christian who thinks he is strong is not merely a hypocrite, he is also a colossal fool. And, unfortunately, a trap for Christian leaders is the tendency to assume that, because of knowledge and position, they are personally strong even though they should know better." (In his classic *The Screwtape Letters,* C.S. Lewis deals with this problem in a humorous, yet penetrating way. It's a "must read.")

The Christian who thinks he is strong is not merely a hypocrite, he is also a colossal fool.

It is important we communicate that every Christian needs to walk in dependence on Jesus and the power of the indwelling Holy Spirit. Inevitably, there will be believers who forget this, and when they do, they will fall on their faces. I reiterate to the unbeliever, that if this did not occasionally happen, I would have to conclude that the Bible is not true.

Occasionally, when you share these truths, someone will say, "It sounds to me like you are trying to use Christianity as a crutch." When someone says this, I chuckle and respond, "Yes, you are right. Christianity is a crutch, and God sent Jesus because there has been an epidemic of broken legs. But remember, the guy who has a broken leg, but refuses to admit it, and tries to walk on it without crutches, is the one who ends up with real bad problems."

Yes, Christianity is a crutch!
Jesus came because there has
been an epidemic of broken legs.

Many years ago, knowing that "the hypocrite charge" was a popular "straw man" used by college students (and sometimes by professors in classrooms) to ridicule Christianity, Campus Crusade included a humorous parody, written anonymously, in an issue of The Collegiate Challenge magazine.

This was during the Vietnam era, and handbills on one subject or another were passed out on campus almost every day. I was ministering in North Carolina, and we made copies of this parody. The students active in our ministry had fun distributing several thousand copies on the campuses of Duke and The University of North Carolina at Chapel Hill.

Our goal was "pre-evangelism," to soften the campuses up a little and to counter the "Christians are hypocrites" objection. I enjoyed this parody so much, that I decided to include it as part of this book. (There is a one sheet copy of this parody in the *Witnessing Letters* packet that can be duplicated.)

I am confident that the anonymous author would be delighted if you use it to help "Make Disciples." It answers the hypocrite question in a unique way, particularly for those who have some knowledge of history.

Keep It Clean!

Once upon a time in a far away land a young man began to announce the discovery of a marvelous kind of soap. People were skeptical at first, but they soon found that this new soap made everyone clean and happy and, because it was so powerful, it got rid of stains that had been around for years.

Because it worked so well, women found that they had more time to spend with their husbands and children. Marriages got better, people were happier, and everyone admired the young man who discovered the soap. The young man refused to charge for the soap and gave it away to all who wanted it. This bothered some rich people, but the poor people loved it. The manufacturers of rival brands of soap became very angry because their business was being hurt badly.

Soon the young man had followers who were traveling all over the country, giving away the new soap to all who wanted it. The new soap was an almost instant success. Thousands became great fans of the new soap, and they formed small groups to spread its use. The other soap manufacturers became desperate and tried to get the young man to charge for his soap, but he refused. He said that it wouldn't be fair to the poor people, and, besides, "My father gave it to me, and He wants it to be free."

When the soap manufacturers found that this strategy wouldn't work, they started a smear campaign against the young man and his followers and their soap. They said the soap made laundry too easy, that you should have to work harder to get things clean. They said that the young man and his followers were immoral and that they had been seen in the company of the dirtiest people in the world. These plans didn't work because the people kept saying "it works, and you can't beat the price."

So finally, the rival soap manufacturers plotted to kill the young man. They paid an informer to betray him and then arrested him. They paid witnesses to perjure themselves in court, and finally they were able to have him convicted and executed. The soap manufacturers were certain that this would take care of their problem, but to their dismay the young man's followers continued to distribute the soap. Persecution didn't work either, for the followers kept spreading to new areas and kept giving away soap.

Finally, the manufacturers decided to try the policy of "if you can't beat them, join them." So they analyzed the young man's soap and came up with a very clever substitute, which looked the same but didn't work. They used the same name for their soap that the young man had used and organized a promotion campaign to corner the market. Because of their organization and advertising, they made great progress and even got many of the followers of the young man to join them for a time.

Soon, however, they started to charge for the soap, and, because their distributors had largely replaced the young man's followers, most people had to buy the soap now, and the substitute really didn't work! Many, however, read of the experience of the early users of the soap and tried to discover where they could get it for free. Several of them were successful, and down through the centuries there was always a group who distributed the soap for free.

After many years, the soap manufacturers decided that they needed a publicity gag to stir up interest in their soap, so they started soap campaigns to go back to the homeland of the young man to try to recover the original bucket in which he had first made the soap. Mighty armies were raised because the homeland of the young man was now in the hands of some people who didn't believe in soap of any kind. These soap campaigns resulted in wars and the deaths of thousands of people and much destruction and heartache. Many campaigns, including children's campaigns, were organized. Many true followers of the young man protested against these campaigns, but they were killed for their efforts. Finally the soap campaigns ceased, but they did stir up a lot of interest and sold a lot of soap.

Several centuries later, when soap sales lagged again, the manufacturers decided to use force to make people buy their soap. They started an intricate system of spies to tell on people who didn't use the right soap, and they used a group of zealous torturers called the Investigation to try people suspected of not using the manufacturers soap. Many people were killed by the Investigation for using the young man's soap, and some for using no soap at all.

Well, hundreds of years have gone by now, and the young man's true soap is still available free, and people are still getting clean and being happy. And there are those who try to peddle a similar but inferior kind of soap for profit and power. There are some, these days, who say that you can't get clean, but that soap is a good thing and everybody ought to have a little, but not go overboard. Others worship books about the original soap, and still others have found that only through its power can they become clean.

Anonymous

Chapter Sixteen

Never, Never, Never Give Up!

Faithful is He that calleth you, who will also do it.
II Thessalonians 5:24

About six months after I left the pastorate of Grace Bible Church in College Station, I received a call at my real estate office from a young woman who said that someone had referred her to me for counsel. I suggested that she drop by my office where we could talk.

When she arrived, Suzanne shared with me that her husband Robert, who worked for a computer company out of Austin, was having an affair with one of his co-workers. Robert and Suzanne had two small children, and she was greatly distressed that her husband was being unfaithful. I asked her if Robert would be willing to meet with me, and she replied, "I don't think so." She paused and then added, "I'm pretty sure he would not."

Not being able to meet with her husband, I was only able to counsel with Suzanne. I began by sharing with her about the forgiveness we have through Jesus death on the cross, and how we are to **"forgive one another, just as God in Christ has forgiven us."** (Ephesians 4:32)

> **Note:** In counseling people, I always begin by dealing with the two sides of forgiveness. First, making sure that they understand the complete and total forgiveness that is available to them through Christ's death on the cross (even many believers don't really grasp this vital truth.) And second, that through the power of the indwelling Holy Spirit, God will give them the spiritual power to forgive the people whom they believe have wronged them. I emphasize that God expects them to forgive others, no

matter what the other person has done (often using the parable of the unjust steward in Matthew 18). Starting with forgiveness deals with the root of problems of guilt and anger, rather than the symptoms. This may be a bit of an overstatement, but I believe, "After dealing with forgiveness, other problems are merely footnotes."

After dealing with forgiveness, other problems are merely footnotes.

After going over forgiveness, I shared, with Suzanne, an experience I had with another couple who had different problems. But, this couple's problems illustrated a vital biblical principle that applies to us all.

Lou was a student at Duke University, and his wife, Jane, was a working wife. They were both Christians. They asked me to come to their apartment one evening as they were having marital problems. That night, when I inquired as to the source of their problems, Lou blurted out, "Jane's mother did this." Jane quickly interrupted and said, "Yes, but his mother did that."

I don't remember what the "this" or "that's" were all about, and it does not really matter. But, for the next fifteen minutes, I listened to a bunch of "this" and "that's" about what each other's mothers had done, and what Jane had done that offended Lou and what Lou had done that offend Jane.

After listening to them, we reviewed the Bible's message of forgiveness, and then suggested that we take a look at a passage in the Bible. I showed them Galatians 5:13-25, and we had a discussion on what it meant to "walk in the Spirit" in contrast to what it meant for a Christian to "walk in the flesh," just like an unbeliever who is not indwelt by the Holy Spirit.

I explained to Lou and Jane, "If we walk yielded to the Holy Spirit, God will give us victory in our lives, in spite of what anyone else does or says to us." In our discussion, I really parked on the difference between the fruit of the flesh and the fruit of the Spirit and indicated that the presence of one or the other in their lives would indicate to them how they are walking.

After sharing with them from Galatians, I turned to Lou and asked, "By the way, tell me again what your mother-in-law did that bothered you?" He gleefully reminded me, and I responded, "Lou, the important question is not what Jane's mother did. The important question is, how did you respond? If you responded in the power of the flesh, I can imagine your response; **disputes, dissensions, strife, outbursts of anger** (from Galatians 5:19-21). However, if you responded by walking in the power of the Holy Spirit, your response would have been **love, joy, peace, longsuffering, gentleness...**" The word *long-suffering* was almost unfair, but I used it anyway.

I then turned to Jane and asked, "Just what was it that his mother did?" She also quickly reminded me. My response to Jane was the same as to Lou. "The important thing is not what the other person did. The important question is, "How did you respond? Was it in the flesh or in the Spirit?"

What the other person did is not important. The important issue is "How did you respond? Was it in the flesh or in the Spirit?"

From that time on in counseling them, I said little other than asking, "What was your response to what the other person did? Was it in the flesh or in the Spirit? If it was in the flesh, I can imagine your response. It was disputes, dissensions, and outbursts of anger. But, if you responded because you were walking in the power of the Holy Spirit, your response was love, joy, peace, longsuffering, gentleness..." This forced both of them to evaluate whether they were walking in the flesh or walking in the Spirit. They responded by learning to "walk in the Spirit" and it did wonders for their marriage.

After telling Suzanne about the victory in Lou's and Jane's lives, I shared with Suzanne that she was going to have to trust the Lord with Robert's life, but that her responsibility was first to forgive him, just as God had forgiven her as a result of what Jesus did for her on the cross.

As with Lou and Jane, the most important thing in her life was not what Robert did or did not do. Rather, the important thing was how she responded to what he did. I said to Suzanne, "Ask yourself, 'Am I responding by the power of the flesh, or by the power of the Holy Spirit who indwells me?' If you respond in the power of the Holy Spirit, the Lord will give you personal victory in your life in spite of anything that Robert does."

I further assured her that if she would trust in the Lord, and walk in the power of the Spirit, that her marriage might be restored. But, if she walked in the flesh, the normal, natural human thing to do, it would do more damage to their marriage, and it was unlikely that it would survive Robert's affair.

I also placed Suzanne in touch with another lady who had followed this counsel in a situation similar to hers, had been victorious, and the Lord had saved her marriage. This lady spent time with Suzanne, shared with her the victory God had given her, and was a real source of encouragement.

Suzanne apparently followed the directions explicitly. Two months later, she told me that she was pregnant again. Robert was still seeing the other woman, and he still would not meet with me.

Over the next several months, Suzanne often called me on the phone, and I continued to remind her that the important thing was not what Robert did, rather the important thing for her was, "Are you walking in the flesh and having disputes, dissension, and outbursts of anger, or walking in the Spirit and having a victorious walk with the Lord?"

Finally, about a month before Suzanne's due date, Robert agreed to meet with me. Suzanne brought Robert to my office, I shared the Gospel with him, and he told me that he was already a Christian.

Robert also agreed to break up with the other woman, but he expressed concern that she did not know Jesus as her Savior. He asked if he could bring the other woman from Austin to meet with me so that I could share the Gospel with her. I consented, and about a week later, Robert and the other woman met me at my office.

After I shared the Gospel with her, Robert told her that he was going to have to break up with her because his wife was having another baby. A battle royal erupted before my eyes. She accused him of bringing her to College Station under false pretenses (which was undoubtedly true), and he insisted that they had to break up. Finally they left my office in a huff.

Robert did break up with the other woman, and Suzanne had the baby. But about a month later, he was back with the other woman. I continued to counsel Suzanne as I had from the beginning, telling her she needed to forgive Robert, just as God had forgiven her, and to walk yielded to the Holy Spirit.

About thirteen months after my first appointment with Suzanne, I got a phone call from her on a Friday evening. She shared with me that the preceding Sunday morning; they had gone to Austin to visit Robert's brother Sam and his wife Katie. While there, they had attended church with Sam and Katie at Allendale Baptist Church, and Robert had walked down the aisle and recommitted his life to Jesus Christ. "But," she continued, "tonight he is with that other woman, and when he comes home, I am not going to be here! I have talked to Sam and Katie about it, and they suggested that I should call you and tell you that I am leaving him."

I replied to Suzanne, "I have never talked to Sam. Can I talk to him?" She said, "I will have him give you a call." A few minutes later, Sam called me from Austin. Sam is a sweet Christian, and he said to me, "I don't know what to think. This is not the first time Robert has done something like this. My friends have seen him around town with that other woman, and I don't know what to do about it."

The next morning, I was scheduled to go to a home by a lake outside of Austin to speak to a training conference for a group of Texas A&M students who were ministering on high school campuses through Young Life. So, I asked Sam if he would go with me and have a man-to-man talk with Robert.

Sam agreed, and I told him I would give him a call after I finished speaking the next morning.

About 11:00 AM the next morning, I called Sam. He told me that he had driven by the other woman's apartment that morning and, sure enough, Robert's Corvette was in the parking lot. I drove to Sam's house, and we headed toward south Austin and her apartment.

Robert's car was not in the parking lot, but we knocked on her door anyway. There was no answer, so we went back to Sam's car and turned on the radio to listen to a football game that had just started in Boston between Texas A&M and Boston College.

After a while, I asked Sam where they worked. He responded, "Back up in the North end of town. We should have gone there first." We drove back to North Austin, and when we drove into the parking lot, there was Robert's Corvette. We parked next to it, and walked into the building to find Robert.

Some men were working on a computer just inside the front door, and we asked them if they knew where Robert Storms was. One of them responded, "I think he is in the back room," and we headed down the hall in the direction he pointed.

As we walked down the hall, the other woman passed us headed in the opposite direction and she really eyeballed us. Unlike the first time we met, I was wearing glasses instead of contacts, and apparently she could not tell for sure whether it was me. When we could not find Robert, someone suggested that maybe he was in a building out back, and we walked back down the hall. Again, we passed the other woman, and again, she again gave us a visual once over.

Not able to find Robert, we pulled out of the parking lot and parked across the street opposite an exit from the parking lot. As we sat in the car, we again turned on the radio. The Texas A&M - Boston College game in Boston was turning into a blowout. Inside the building, Robert was stewing in his juices.

Finally, Robert picked up a phone, called Suzanne in College Station and asked, "Sam and some guy were here in

Austin looking for me. Who is with Sam?" She responded, "Our little boy just got in an ant hill and I have to take him to the doctor. Go find out for yourself," and she hung up the phone.

The game on the radio ended with the Aggies beating Boston College by a score of 37 to 2, and Sam decided to sneak through the woods next to the building to see if he could spot Robert. A few minutes later, he came running back and said, "They just walked out of the building and are headed toward his car. What shall we do?" I suggested that we did not want to get involved in a high-speed chase with Robert in a Corvette and us in an Olds 98, so Sam jumped behind the wheel and we drove into the parking lot.

We pulled up next to Robert's Corvette (it had the top down), I rolled down my window, and before we could say anything, Robert said, "I heard you guys were looking for me." I responded, "Robert, we love you, we are concerned for you, and we want to have a talk." He said, "O.K. Let's talk." I responded, "No Robert, we don't want to talk to you here, we want to go to a coffee shop where we can have some privacy, and talk to you there." Robert replied, "O.K., we will follow you."

At that point, older brother Sam interrupted, "No Robert, we don't want to talk to both of you. We want to talk to you alone. We want you to get out of that car, we want you to get into this car, and we want you to do it RIGHT NOW!" Robert said to the other woman, "Well, at least I should talk to them. I will meet you later." He got out of his Corvette, put up the top and got into the back seat of Sam's car.

It was a very quiet ride down the freeway to a Denny's restaurant. We found a booth in the back and sat down. Robert looked at me and said, "Boy, I hope you didn't have to come all the way from College Station just for this." I explained to him that I didn't, that I was there to speak at a Young Life gathering. Then I said, "Robert, we love you and we are concerned for you, we are concerned for Suzanne, we are concerned for the other woman (I forget her name), and most important of all, I am concerned for three little kids who want to have a daddy." Then I opened my Bible and read to him from Hebrews chapter ten about the consequences of going on sinning after coming to a knowledge of the truth.

As the conversation progressed, I said, "You know Robert, you asked if I had to come to Austin just for this, and I responded, no. But Robert, I came here to speak to a Young Life group that wanted to go to Galveston. Nothing would work out for them, so they finally decided to have their conference at one of their homes out by Lake Travis. Robert, the Lord had to bring forty people to Austin so I could talk to you." Then I said, "Robert, you think that you would be happy if you left your wife and hooked up with that other woman. But, that is not a solution, because there will be another and another and another."

Robert finally looked at me and said, "I know that everything you have said is true. But when I get around that woman, I am like putty in her hands." I admitted to Robert, "I made a big mistake when we went though this earlier. You thought you were strong enough to continue working at the same company with her, and I did not discourage you. I was wrong. You need to quit your job and never see that woman again."

Robert asked, "Do one of you have a quarter? I need to call my boss." Sam gave him a quarter, Robert went to the phone, came back about five minutes later, and said, "My boss is going to get a hair cut in a half hour, and he said I can meet him at the barbershop." Robert was wearing swimming trunks and he asked Sam if we could go to his house and borrow a pair of pants." Sam said "sure."

We drove back to Robert's car. Sam got out of his car, moved into the driver's seat of Robert's Corvette, and drove Robert to his home. I followed in the Olds 98. After Robert changed clothing, he headed toward the door, and Sam asked, "Can I go along?" Robert said, "Sure," and they drove to the barber shop where Robert quit his job.

When they returned, Sam, Katie, Robert, and I were sitting in their living room, and I will never forget our conversation. Sam said, "You know, Robert, I'm not much with words. But, when I have a temptation, there is a verse that I like to think about. I don't know if I am interpreting it correctly, but it really helps me."

Sam read Hebrews 12:1, **"Therefore, since we have so great a cloud of witnesses surrounding us, let us lay aside every encumbrance, and the sin which so easily entangles us, and let us run with endurance the race that is set before us."** Then Sam continued, "You know, Robert, when I have a temptation, I like to think about our parents in heaven, that they are watching. Robert, I remember when I was only five years old and you were still in our mother's womb. We were in Tokyo, and I was a coward. I stayed back by the luggage and would not even go out to the plane when our dad got on it to fly off to Korea. As you know, Dad was killed in Korea and never returned."

"Robert, the Lord provided for us as our mother took care of four little boys. I remember when everyone else's oranges froze down in the valley and ours were not even touched. Then mom came down with cancer. We prayed, and the Lord allowed her to stay with us for another year and a half. Then she went to be with our father who was already in heaven. Robert, I like to think that they are both up there watching us."

By the time Sam finished, Katie was crying, Sam and Robert both had tears coming down their cheeks, and I must admit that I was misty eyed. All of a sudden, Robert jumped from his chair, raced over to the phone and called Suzanne in College Station. He asked her, "How is our little boy?" She answered, "He is O.K.," and Robert said, "I will be home in a few hours."

When Robert rejoined us, he said, "I have one more problem. All of my clothes are over at her house." Sam looked at Robert and said, "I guess that is what brothers are for."

I asked Robert what the other woman's schedule was for the rest of the day. He explained that she had to host a party away from her apartment at 7:00 that evening. I said to Robert, "I have to go back and speak again to the Young Life group, so I can't go with you. Wait until 7:30, call her apartment and be sure she does not answer. Have Sam go with you, drive through the parking lot to be sure her car is not there, and then use the key she gave you. Get your clothes, and get out of there fast."

They followed my instructions, and Katie went along with them. No one answered the other woman's phone, and her car was not in the parking lot. Robert used the key to open the door, and there she was waiting for him. She yelled at him, "It's about time you got here!" An argument followed, and Robert got upset because she had hidden his shaving kit.

As the battle went on, Katie used the other woman's phone to call some ladies in her church to get them to activate their prayer chain. Finally, Robert found his shaving kit, they got in Sam's car, and had to almost run the other woman down to get out of the parking lot. They were all so shook up over the confrontation, that they drove straight to Harold O'Chester's home. (Harold was Sam and Katie's pastor at Allendale Baptist Church).

Before I started writing this chapter, I called Robert and Suzanne on the phone, and they are doing great. Right off of the top of his head, Robert said, "The day it all happened was September 9, 1978. That's the day that I became a Christian." Since that time, Robert has pastored two different churches. As of the writing of this book, he is the manager of a public housing project in Brenham, Texas, and for him, it provides an opportunity to minister. Suzanne now works in a Christian book store, and I'm hoping that she will push this book when it makes it to the shelves.

Several years after "the day," Robert and Suzanne moved to Austin and became active in Allendale Baptist Church (it has since changed its name to Great Hills Baptist Church). The church sponsored a series of Sunday morning Marriage Enrichment Seminars at a nearby hotel. They advertised the seminars in a local newspaper, and it had become a very effective evangelistic outreach. One of the important parts of each seminar was when Robert and Suzanne shared their testimonies, and they told how God had healed their marriage and made it better than ever.

Great Hills Baptist Church held a seminar for people from other churches to explain how to hold similar marriage conferences near their churches, and I was asked to attend. That day, I got to hear both Robert and Suzanne give their testimonies, and it was a rich blessing for me.

At the end of the seminar, I was asked to share a few words. As I thought back on what the Lord had done, I commented,

"From a human viewpoint, I should have told Suzanne to leave Robert, that he would never change. But, I did not because Suzanne continued to seek my counsel, and I was not about to be the first person to give up hope.

I then recalled a speech by Winston Churchill during a dark period of the Second World War. He was given an impressive introduction, but when he walked up to the podium, he looked over the crowd and said, "Never give up! Never give up! Never, never, never, give up!" And ... He sat down. (And, so did I.)

A few years ago, over fifteen years after "the day," Robert and I had lunch with a friend in College Station. As we shared the story about how the Lord had worked a miracle in Robert's life, I mentioned that someone in Austin had suggested that Suzanne call me for counsel.

Robert interrupted, "Oh no! That's not how it happened." Then he explained that Suzanne had gone to the Southern Baptist Association office in Bryan-College Station, explained what her problem was, and asked for someone to counsel her. The secretary suggested that she go see the pastor at Grace Bible Church, which was not a member of the association.

Suzanne then drove across town to Grace Bible Church, knocked on the door, and no one was there. A college student from the apartments next door noticed her knocking on the door, walked over from her apartment, and asked her who she was looking for. Suzanne explained that she needed to talk to the pastor. The coed said, "This church has a new pastor. You are probably looking for the former pastor. He is now in the real estate business," and she handed her my phone number on a piece of paper.

As I write about this I get goose bumps. God knew that He was going to have me in Austin on "the day." He moved the secretary at the Baptist association office to send Suzanne to a church that was not a part of the association where she was employed.

Then there was the college student. Obviously she was walking in the power of the Holy Spirit when God lead her to give Suzanne my phone number. I hope that she reads this book sometime and learns how she was used by the Lord. For sure, she will find out in Glory.

If you are prepared and available, God will know it. He can move secretaries, students who live nearby, and even mountains to bring you into contact with the people He wants you to reach with the Gospel.

If you are prepared and available, God will know it, and He can lead you to make contact with people whom He wants you to reach with the Gospel.

So, prepare yourself to be effective when you share your faith, get ready for some blessings, and remember ...

"As you are going ... make disciples," and never, never, never, give up!

Chapter Seventeen

No Vestigial Christians

For as we have many members in one body, and all members have not the same office: So we, being many, are one body in Christ, and every one members one of another.
Romans 12:4-5

Longfellow wrote in his Psalm of Life, "Lives of great men all remind us, we can live our lives sublime. And departing leave behind us foot prints in the sands of time." To close this book, we will look at the lives of two men who left footprints in the sands of time.

The first is Russell H. Conwell. After the civil war, Conwell attended law school and eventually settled in Boston where he had a lucrative law practice. As an attorney, he was asked to meet with the leaders of a church in suburban Lexington, to explain to them how to close the doors of a dying church and dispose of its property. At the meeting, Russell H. Conwell suggested that they should try one more time to revive the church, and he offered to come out to the church for a workday, and help them fix up their old run down building.

They all agreed to have the work day on the following Saturday. But, Conwell was the only one who showed up. He had an ax with him, so he started to chop off the rickety front steps. As he was chopping, a man walked by and asked, "What are you doing?" Conwell responded, "We are going to tear down this church and build a new one." The man responded, "The people won't do that." Conwell said, "Yes they will!" and he kept chopping. The man watched for a few minutes, and then he said, "I will contribute $100 dollars. Stop by my livery stable up the street and I will give you the money tonight."

Conwell kept chopping on the church steps, and a little

later, another man stopped to watch him and also asked, "What are you doing." Conwell again explained that they were going to build a new church. The man replied, "That's ridiculous. No one will contribute to rebuild this old church." Conwell said, "The owner of that livery stable up the street just said he will give one hundred dollars." The man replied, "He would not do that. He does not even go to church, let alone this one." Conwell said nothing; he just kept chopping. The man started to walk away, then turned back and said, "Well, if he does, I will match it with another hundred dollars."

Conwell went to the people in the church and told them about the contributions. Two hundred dollars was a lot of money back in the 19th century, when a loaf of bread cost less than a nickel, so the people decided to move forward with the new church. To help out more, Russell H. Conwell started to fill their pulpit as they could not afford a preacher, and in 1879 he left his law practice and became the pastor of that church in Lexington.

Under Conwell's leadership, the church in Lexington grew and prospered. A few years later, Conwell accepted the call to pastor Grace Baptist Church, a struggling congregation in a poor section of Philadelphia, even though he had to take a cut in pay. This church grew so quickly that one Sunday morning, when Conwell arrived at the church, a group of children were waiting outside. There was a little girl in the group, named Hattie May Wiatt, whom Conwell knew well because she lived near the church. Conwell picked her up and asked her what the problem was. She replied that her Sunday School class was so full that there was no room for her.

The next day, as Conwell walked to the church, he crossed paths with Hattie as she was walking to school, and he told her that, when they raised the money, they would have a new room for her Sunday School class that would be big enough so that no one would be turned away.

Unbeknown to Russell H. Conwell, Hattie started saving pennies for the new Sunday School building. A few months later, Hattie got sick and died. At her funeral, her parents gave Conwell a sack with 57 cents in it -- pennies that Hattie had saved for the new Sunday School building.

With the 57 cents in his hand, Conwell went to his church, told them about Hattie, and offered the 57 pennies for sale to raise money for a Sunday School building. They were bought by member of the church for $250, enough to purchase a home next to the church. Fifty-four of the members who purchased pennies returned them as contributions to the church, and Conwell had them put in a frame as a remembrance.

As the church continued to grow, they needed more facilities, but Grace Baptist Church was heavily in debt. Conwell approached the owner of the parcel of land they desired, and asked him to hold it for them until they could afford to purchase it. After hearing about Hattie, the owner agreed to sell it to them for $25,000. He asked for a down payment -- 54 pennies, with the balance to be paid with 5% interest.

When completed, the church built on that parcel of ground, bought with a down payment from the heart of that little girl, was the largest church in the United States in that day. It was a church that would seat over 4,000 people, large enough so that no one would be turned away. Since a large contributor would not let the building be called a church until all debt was retired, it was called Baptist Temple, a name that stuck. It should be noted, the gentleman who sold them the land made a contribution of 54 cents to help build the new church.

Conwell's expressed the goal and purpose of the Baptist Temple as follows:

> "The mission of the church is to save the souls of men. That is its true mission.... We are here to save the souls of dying sinners; we are here for no other purpose; and the mission of the church being so clear, that is the only test of a real church."

In 1884, a young man came to Conwell for counsel. He wanted to become a minister, but could not afford to go to college. Conwell offered to personally teach him one evening a week. The young man asked if he could bring a few friends, and Conwell agreed. Six young men showed up for the first night class. It was held in the house purchased with the $250 from the sale of 57 pennies. By the third class, it numbered forty. From that start, over 100,000 students had attended Temple College, later incorporated as Temple University, before Conwell retired as its president 38 years later. In 1965 Temple University was acquired by the State of Pennsylvania and in 1969 the Conwell School of Theology (at one time part of Temple University) and Gordon Divinity School merged and became Gordon-Conwell Theological Seminary.

There was a poor lady in the church who became ill, but could not afford to go to the hospital. The church rented a room in a nearby rooming house, and hired a practical nurse to care for her. Then there was another, and another, and they rented more rooms. This meager start eventually became the Samaritan Hospital. Before Russell H. Conwell retired as President of the hospital, it had treated over 400,000 patients. Today it is the Temple University Hospital and Medical School.

Russell H. Conwell was most well known for a lecture titled *The Acres of Diamonds*. During his life, he gave this lecture over 6000 times, in cities large and small across America, and he made several million dollars delivering it. This was an amazing feat when one considers that Conwell was middle aged before the first horseless carriage was invented, and sixty years old when the Wright Brothers first flew the Kitty Hawk. Apparently Conwell spent a lot of time writing on trains, as he was also the author of 40 books.

The lecture started with a story about a man who sold his farm to go looking for diamonds, and after he died they found acres of diamond on the farm he sold. The theme of the message was that you can find your wealth right where you are, and it is a good thing to be industrious and make a lot of money, as long as you use it properly. In today's jargon, you could say that Russell H. Conwell was the leading spin-doctor for the industrial revolution. In 1914, when Russell H. Conwell delivered the lecture for the five thousandth time, dignitaries from all over the country attended, including the governors from nine states.

Conwell practiced what he preached. He never kept a dime of the money from his lectures. After each presentation, Conwell would deduct his expenses from the honorarium, and write several personal letters to young men working their way through college. The names of these young men were supplied to him by ministers and college professors. Conwell included a check with each letter, and told the young men that he did not want to know how they used the money, that their only responsibility was to the Lord.

The ministries of the church in Lexington and the Baptist Temple in Philadelphia, Temple University, the Samaritan Hospital, the many people he inspired to succeed by his lectures and books, and the lives of each of those young men were all footprints that Russell H. Conwell left in the sands of time.

Johnnie Ring looked like a small lad

The second man I want to tell you about was quite different from Conwell. While Conwell was tall and impressive, Johnnie Ring looked like a small lad. When the civil war broke out, Johnnie Ring wanted to join the army and fight for the Union side. He tried to enlist, but was rejected. They said that he was too small.

Finally, Johnnie did get accepted, but only as an orderly for a captain in a local artillery company. The men in this company were devoted to their captain, and, before going into battle, they bought a sword for him and had the Latin words for "True friendship is eternal" engraved on its silver and gold scabbard.

To Johnnie Ring, this sword represented the honor of battle. Every night he would take it off of the center post in the captain's tent and polish it. Johnnie was also a very strong Christian, and every night he read his Bible in the Captain's tent. The captain was an atheist, and he laughed at Johnnie for reading his bible and praying. This led Johnnie to read his Bible outside of the Captain's tent to avoid being the subject of his captain's jokes. But Johnnie was faithful to his Lord, and he continued to read his Bible and pray -- in spite of his captain's kidding.

One day, the artillery unit was about to be overrun by the army of the south, and they retreated across a river using an old wooden bridge. When they got to the other side, Johnnie ran up to a sergeant and asked, "Where's the captains sword?" The sergeant responded, "It's in his tent where he always leaves it." Johnnie Ring instantly turned, and ran back across the bridge. He weaved his way through the men of the south undetected, as he looked like a small boy. When he got to the captains tent, he grabbed the sword, and headed back toward the bridge. But, when he got to the edge of the river, the bridge had been set on fire by the men of the North, so that the Rebel army could not pursue them.

With the sword in his hand, Johnnie Ring started across that blazing bridge. Both the men and of the North and the men of the South spotted him on the bridge as the gunfire continued. Every few steps, he would try to stick his head over the edge of the bridge to get a breath of fresh air. Finally, an officer from the south ran down to the edge of the river, waved a white handkerchief and the gunfire stopped. He yelled to Johnnie, "Come back, we will let you go free." The soldiers from both sides ran down to the edge of the river and began shouting at him. The men of the North yelled, "Go back, you can't make it." The men of the South yelled, "Come Back, we will let you go free! Come Back! Come Back!"

But Johnnie Ring could not hear them because of the roar of the blaze, and he kept moving forward through the blazing inferno. When Johnnie disappeared into the covered portion of the bridge, the battlefield went silent except for the crackling of the fire. Then both sides cheered when he appeared on the other side, though his clothes were aflame. When Johnnie reached the end of the bridge, he fell off into the water, the men of the North pulled him out of the river, put him on a gun carriage, and took him back to an army hospital.

A few days later, Johnnie Ring died. But, before he died, he said, "Give the captain his sword." The captain remembered the life of Johnnie Ring, and remembered that he was a strong Christian. Before that war was over, the Captain became a Christian because of his remembrance of the faithful witness of Johnnie Ring. The only footprint that Johnnie Ring left in the sands of time was the life of his captain. Johnnie Ring's captain was Russell H. Conwell.

I first heard about Russell H. Conwell and Johnnie Ring from my father, Clyde Prall. As a young man, he attended the Baptist Temple in Philadelphia, and he told me about an inspirational meeting he attended at the church. It was late in Conwell's life, and they asked him to tell again the story of *Johnnie Ring and the Captain's Sword.*

The church was full, and Conwell was a great orator. Just as he had everyone on the edge of their seats, as he was telling of Johnnie Ring crossing the blazing bridge, an old gentleman sitting on the front row, wearing a rebel hat, jumped to his feet and in his excitement, he let out a Rebel yell, and shouted, "The story is true, the whole story is true! I know; I was there on the side of the South."

This reminds us of another story that is true. Yes, the whole story is true. It's the greatest story ever told. **"For God so love the world that He gave His only begotten Son, that whosoever believeth in Him would not perish but have everlasting life."**

But, do you have I John 3:16 memorized?

You probably have John 3:16 memorized. But, do you have I John 3:16 memorized? Read it carefully; **"By this we know love, that He laid down His life for us, and we ought to lay down our lives for the brethren."** Read it again, and please mentally personalize it for your own life. **"By this I know love, that He laid down His life for me, and I ought to lay down my life for the brethren."**

The rest of his life, Russell H. Conwell greatly valued that sword. He kept it in his bedroom. Each morning when he awakened, Conwell would look at the sword and he would repeat a vow, "Today I am going to work sixteen hours, eight hours for myself and eight hours for Johnnie Ring."

Just as Russell H. Conwell was reminded that Johnny Ring laid down his life for him, when he looked at the sword in the silver and gold scabbard, so also, every time we see a cross, we need to remember that Jesus Christ laid down His life for us, and that we ought to lay down our lives for the brethren.

But, you ask, "Why the brethren?" Wouldn't it be more appropriate that I lay down my life for Jesus Christ? After all, it was Jesus who died for me, not the brethren.

Please consider Romans chapter 12:3-8: **"For through the grace that was given to me I say to every man among you not to think more highly of himself than he ought to think, but to think so as to have sound judgment, as God has allotted to each a measure of faith. For just as we have many members in one body and all members do not have the same function, so we, who are many, are one body in Christ, and individually members one of another. And since we have gifts that differ according to the grace given to us, *let us exercise them accordingly*: if prophecy according to the proportion of his faith; if service, in his serving; or he who teaches, in his teaching; or he who exhorts, in his exhortation; he who gives, with liberality; he who leads. with diligence, he who shows mercy, with cheerfulness."**

Also consider Ephesians 4:4-8 & 11-16: **"There is one body and one Spirit, just as also you were called in one hope of your calling, one Lord, one faith, one baptism, one God and Father of all who is over all and through all in all. But to each one of us was given according to the measure of Christ's gift, therefore it says, 'Where He ascended on high, He led captive a host of captives, and He gave gifts to men.'"**

"And He gave some as apostles, and some as prophets, and some as evangelists, and some as pastors and teachers, for the equipping of the saints for the work of service to the building up of the body of Christ; until we all attain to the unity of the faith, and of the knowledge of the Son of God, to a mature man, to the measure of the stature which belongs to the fullness of Christ. As a result, we are no longer to be children, tossed here and there by waves, and carried about by every wind of doctrine, by the trickery of men, by craftiness in deceitful scheming; but speaking the truth in love, we are to grow up in all aspects into Him, who is the head, even Christ, from whom the whole body, being fitted and held together by that which every joint supplies, according to the proper working of each individual part, causes the growth of the body for the building up of itself in love."

The reason that the Apostle John said we need to lay down our lives for the brethren, instead of saying we should lay it down for Jesus Christ, is because "the brethren," "the church," is the body of Jesus Christ on earth today. Yes, the Church is the body that Jesus Christ now uses to minister to believers and to reach the lost. While there is an application that we should lay down our lives for the Church universal, all true believers, the primary way that God works in the world today is though local churches, through local bodies of believers.

Your local church is a body of Jesus Christ.

Your local church is a body of Jesus Christ. The head of your church is not your senior pastor. The head of your church is Jesus Christ. Your pastor is merely the under-shepherd. And, each member of His church is part of His body.

Yes, God calls some people to have particularly significant functions in the body, but Paul's emphasis is that for the body to function properly, every individual part must fulfill its assigned purpose. Think again about Ephesians 4:16 **"from whom the whole body, joined and knit together by what every joint supplies..."**

It was thought that tonsils and appendix had no function in the human body, that they were merely a vestige of history.

When I was a youth, it was taught that tonsils and appendix had no function in the human body. They were called vestigial organs, and these so called vestigial organs were used as evidence to support the evolutionary hypothesis. They were called vestigial because they were considered a vestige of the evolutionary development of our bodies, merely leftovers from history.

Further research has established that every organ in the human body has a function. When God created your physical body, He did not give it organs that have no function or purpose, and there are no vestigial organs in the body of Jesus Christ. God did not save you so that you can be a vestigial Christian. We all have Spiritual gifts that we are to exercise as members of His body.

Now, some may be ask, "What are my spiritual gifts? In recent years, there have been many books written on how to discover your Spiritual gifts, and there are Christian leaders that hold seminars on the subject. As a matter of fact, I have a seminar titled *How to Discover your Spiritual Gifts.* In my seminar, I teach everything I know about the subject. Consequently, mine is a two-minute seminar. Consider yourself enrolled, and be a participant in my seminar right now:

> First, ask yourself a question. "If I knew what my Spiritual gifts are, would I exercise them for the benefit of the brethren in my local church?" Please write down your answer in the margin. Write "Y" for *yes,* "N" for *no,* or "D" for that *depends* on what it is and how much of my precious time it will consume. If you have written down "Y" for yes, and you really mean it, God will reveal your gift to you.
>
> Don't ask me how He will revel your gifts to you. Paul wrote in Romans 11, **"Oh the wealth of the riches both of the wisdom and knowledge of God. How unsearchable are His judgments and His ways past finding out."** So, I don't have an answer to your how questions. I do have a hunch about your Spiritual gifts. My guess is that they will be things that you really enjoy doing.
>
> But, let me assure you. If you are willing to use your gifts for the benefit of the brethren, God will make sure that you know what they are. On the other hand, if you merely want to know what your gifts are for personal edification or self-aggrandizement, don't waste a lot of time trying to discover them. It will be a futile search.
>
> So, let me close this seminar with a summary: "If you knew it, would you use it? If you would, YOU WILL KNOW IT!"

Seminar concluded. You now know everything I know about discovering Spiritual gifts.

Let's review a bit. We are all part of one body, the body of Christ, and the Bible teaches us that God has given each of us gifts that we should exercise for the benefit of the whole body, our brethren in Christ. We all have different functions, and we each fulfill different needs in His body by exercising our gifts.

Working together as members of the Body of Jesus Christ, God wants to use us to seek and save the lost.

Working together as members of the Body of Jesus Christ, God wants us to fulfill His mission to seek and save the lost. Jesus gave us that mission in the Great Commission in Matthew 28. The marching orders for His Body are to make disciples. God may not call you to go overseas as a missionary. But, as part of His body, He has called you to contribute to the process of making disciples wherever you are, today, and for the rest of your life here on earth. Again, there are no vestigial organs in the Body of Jesus Christ.

While we each may have a primary motivational gift, God's gifting of us can also be a process. One may be a gifted teacher, but to exercise that gift he, or she, needs to study and prepare. And, it can be a life long process. It certainly has been for me.

I came to know Christ a couple of years after graduating from the University of Oregon. Six months after accepting Christ, by God's grace I found myself back in school as a student at Western Seminary in Portland. As a new believer, I did not have the biblical background that many of my fellow students possessed, and I sensed that I needed to get a grasp on the Biblical big picture so that I could better understand the individual parts. A seminary professor suggested several books to help me accomplish this goal, and the summer after my first year at seminary, I devoured a couple of the six hundred page books that he recommended.

After graduating from Western Seminary, I joined the staff of Campus Crusade for Christ. As mentioned in Chapter One, Campus Crusade had just purchased an old resort hotel called

Arrowhead Springs in San Bernardino, California, and each week we had a series of rotating, one hour seminars as part of the Leadership Training Institutes. As a seminary graduate, I kept getting assigned the seminar titled "Bible Overview."

Since I only had an hour to work with, and a lot of material to cover, I told the students to close their Bibles and I would talk them through the biblical big picture. Some weeks I taught it five or six times. Since then, I have expanded it into various formats and have probably taught the content of those seminars, in one form or another, over fifty times. Then, several years ago, my son told me I was going to be a grandfather, so I put it in book form for my grand children, and titled it ***The Master Plot of the Bible.***

Having the book, and being a part of His body, the Lord has now gifted me with a unique evangelism ministry to help "make disciples." To introduce it, let me ask a few questions: "Have you ever received a letter in the mail that tried to sell you life insurance?" Of course you all have. "But, have you ever received a letter in the mail that explained how you could get eternal life assurance -- the Gospel?" I have asked this question of many believers. They have all received letters to invite them to meetings, and most have received fund raising appeals. But, none have recalled receiving a letter that made a clear presentation of the Gospel.

In our ministry at Emmaus Books, we have individuals and churches send us names and addresses, and we send out a series of four evangelism letters, in about two week intervals. These letters present the Gospel and Christian evidences, and each one includes a gift certificate for a free copy of *The Master Plot of the Bible.* We send the book to responders, postage paid. The cover sheets for the church sponsored letters tell the recipient that they are compliments of the sponsoring church and the church's address in our web page the *Bride of Christ Church Directory* is also included (more info at www.hisbride.org.)

Now notice a very important truth. Without help from other parts of the Body of Jesus Christ, our ministry will fail. If other parts of the Body of Christ do not supply us with the names, and the resources, our efforts will be a total waste of time.

If we send out my letters, and book, and a recipient responds by accepting Christ, I know that in God's eyes the person, who submitted the name, and those who prayed, are a vital part of that person becoming a Christian. We are all part of ONE BODY. Again, the biblical principal is that "Some plant, others water, but God brings the increase."

We are all part of one body.

I Corinthians, Chapter 12, is another chapter that deals with Spiritual gifts. Verse 4 reads, **"There are a variety of Gifts but the same Spirit."** Verse 7 reads, **"But to each one is given a manifestation of the Spirit for the profit of all."** Verse 11 reads, **"But one and the same Spirit works all things, distributing to each one individually just as He wills."** Verse 18 reads, **"But now God has placed the members, each of them, in the body, as He desires."** Verse 22 reads, **"On the contrary, it is much truer that the members of the body which seem to be weaker are necessary."** And, verse 25 reads, **"that here should be no division in the body, but that the members should have the same care for one another"**

These verses focus on the main teachings that Paul gives us about Spiritual gifts. There are a diversity of gifts, we all have different gifts, and our gifts are given to us for the benefit of the whole body, so that it can function properly. It's important to remember that God the Holy Spirit determines who should have what gifts. He distributes the gifts as He wills, not as we will. And, every part of the body is needed for the body to function properly. Remember, the Body of Christ has no vestigial organs, and God does not want you to be a vestigial Christian.

Every part of His Body is vital. While we have focused on evangelism in this book, and making disciples does begin with a new spiritual birth, discipleship is also an ongoing process. Just as every member of a family can be involved in the physical and emotional growth of a newborn child, so also every member of a local church can be part of the nurturing of new believers. Discipleship is more than merely imparting knowledge. The loving support and fellowship of the whole body of believers can be one of the major factors in the spiritual growth of a new believer.

To fulfill our calling, the parts of a local body of believers needs to work harmoniously, motivated by love for the brethren. Always remember, if you are properly exercising your spiritual gifts, they will contribute to spiritual unity in the body.

When thinking about how a local Church should function, I like to compare it to a football team. A football team has a variety of positions, and each member of the team must play his position properly for his team to be a winner. The offensive linemen need to block, the linebackers need to tackle, and everyone can't be a running back or the quarterback.

There is not a lot of glory passed around to offensive linemen. But, let me assure you, every head coach, and I should add, every quarterback and running back, knows their value. They are vital to the team's success. In fact, every member of a football team must fulfill his part for the team to accomplish its goals. And, a winning team must be unified, or as football junkies put it, to have a winner, a team needs "good chemistry."

During my senior year at the University of Oregon, our football team had great team chemistry. The next to last game on our schedule was at Washington State. The game was to determine who would go to the Rose Bowl. If we won, Oregon would go, but if Washington State tied the game, they would go.

At the last minute, a fraternity brother, who was a member of the team, but was not making the trip because of an injury, talked me into driving up to Pullman for the game. The game was a sellout. But, since Larry was a team member, we just went in with the team and watched the game from the sidelines.

During the game, I could not help but notice a player named John. He was a senior, but he never got in the game. John constantly worked the bench. When players came out of the game, John was there telling them what a great job they were doing, and when they were headed back into the game, John was there encouraging them.

Oregon went ahead by fourteen points early in the game, and then Washington State made a big comeback. When the score was 14 to 7 late in the game, and Washington State was driving for another touchdown, our bench was going crazy. But, John was keeping his cool and continued to encourage his teammates. Washington State did score, but missed their extra point, so we won and Oregon played in the 1958 Rose bowl.

On the drive back to Eugene, I discussed John's contribution to the team with my fraternity brother. Larry explained, "John is a receiver who is not very fast, so he doesn't get to play much, but he is the inspirational leader for our team from the bench."

John didn't get a lot of glory for his contribution from the bench. He had been a star in high school, but he rarely got in the game at the University of Oregon. I think he made a token appearance in our Rose Bowl game, but it was probably for only a play or two, because it was a close game. Ohio State won by 10 to 7.

There is no doubt that many football players have a different attitude than John. They have a bad case of "What's in it for me?" with no loyalty to the team. Some say, "If I can't be a star on this team, I'm out of here." Others will stick it out, even if they don't get to play, to get a free education. But they have had a bad attitude, a critical spirit, and often cause division on their team."

This is more of a problem for football coaches today than it was forty years ago when I was in college. A lot of older coaches have difficulty in adjusting to the free spirit, lack of loyalty, undisciplined attitude, that is prevalent in much of our society today.

Football coaches are not the only ones confronted with this problem. The same attitudes have infected many American Christians. In our mobile society, many believers have shallow roots in their local church. They have a "What's in it for me?" attitude, with no real deep-seated loyalty to the Body. If everything does not fit them to a "T," they say, "I'm out of here!'

And, when they look for a new church home, it's like they are shopping for a new car with a "Where can I find the best deal for me and my family" approach. And when they do join a church, they act like it's a spectator sport -- like a football game where there are 22 men on the field, desperately in need of rest, and 50,000 in the stands desperately in need of exercise.

But John, the University of Oregon bench warmer, had a great attitude. He spent four years as a loyal member of the team, not complaining, and humbly using his gift of encouragement on the sidelines. Len Cassanova, the Oregon head coach, was fully aware of John's loyal contribution to the team. After John graduated, he rewarded him. One year out of college, he hired John to be a full time assistant coach at the University of Oregon.

For twelve years John loyally served as an assistant coach at the University of Oregon. Later, when one of our other assistant coaches became the head coach at another college, he hired John away from us. Some years later, when that coach resigned, John replaced him as the head coach.

John was a good head coach. During his tenure at the University of Southern California, John Robinson's teams won four Rose Bowls and one national championship. Later, as a head coach in the NFL, John Robinson's Rams won their way to the conference finals two times, just one game short of the Super Bowl. And it all started because John Robinson was a faithful encourager, when he was what many would call "a bench warmer."

As a believer, you are a member of a team; it's called a local church -- a Body of Jesus Christ. The Lord is your head coach (your pastor is the offensive coordinator). The Lord knows whether you are fulfilling your calling as a member of His body, or whether you are goofing off on the sidelines. He has promised that He will reward you, if you are faithful.

I Corinthians 3:11-15 tells us that each one of us are in the process of building a life structure. It's either composed of gold, silver and precious stones -- actions and attitudes with great value, or wood, hay, and stubble -- actions and attitudes with very little value. And, Paul tells us that God will reward our faithfulness:

> **"For no man can lay a foundation other than the one which is laid, which is Jesus Christ. Now if any man builds upon the foundation with gold, silver, and precious stones, wood, hay, straw, each man's work will become evident; for the day will show it, because it is to be revealed with fire; and the fire itself will test the quality of each man's work. If any man's work which he has built upon it remains, he shall receive a reward. If any man's work is burned up, he shall suffer loss, but he himself shall be saved, yet so as through fire."**

There is also an awesome declaration in Daniel 12:2-3:

> **And many of those who sleep in the dust of the earth will awake, these to everlasting life, but others to disgrace and everlasting contempt. And those who have insight will shine brightly like the brightness of the expanse of heaven, and those who lead many to righteousness, like the stars forever and ever.**

This life will soon pass for all of us. You are not a vestigial organ in the body of Jesus Christ. Now is the time to prepare for eternity. Use your God given gifts and talents to help His body, the church, accomplish its mission in this world. And, whenever you see a cross, recall and personalize I John 3:16: "**By this I know love, that He laid down His life for me, and I ought to lay down my life for the brethren.**"

As a member of His team, Jesus wants you to be a vital part of His game plan. So --

As You are Going... Make Disciples...